Dinner in One

Melissa Clark
Dinner in One

Exceptional & Easy One-Pan Meals

Photographs by Linda Xiao

CLARKSON POTTER/PUBLISHERS
New York

Published in the United States by
Clarkson Potter/Publishers,
an imprint of Random House,
a division of Penguin Random House LLC,
New York.
clarksonpotter.com

CLARKSON POTTER is a trademark
and POTTER with colophon
is a registered trademark of
Penguin Random House LLC.

Library of Congress Cataloging-in-
Publication Data is available
upon request.

ISBN 978-0-593-23325-2
Ebook ISBN 978-0-593-23326-9

Printed in China

Editor: Doris Cooper
Art Director & Designer:
Stephanie Huntwork
Photographer: Linda Xiao
Photography Assistant: Christina Zhang
Food Stylists: Monica Pierini and
Emma Rowe
Prop Stylists: Paige Hicks and
Julie Bernouis
Production Manager: Kim Tyner
Production Editor: Terry Deal
Copy Editor: Rachel Holzman
Indexer: Thérèse Shere
Marketer: Stephanie Davis
Publicist: Erica Gelbard

10 9 8 7 6 5 4 3 2 1

First Edition

For my mother, Rita,
whose commitment to
being clear-eyed—in the
kitchen and in life—is a
constant inspiration

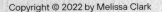

CHEESY BAKED PASTA WITH TOMATO, SAUSAGE, AND RICOTTA, PAGE 106

Contents

One-Pot Pastas & Noodles 105

Dutch Ovens 132

Casseroles 155

Soup Pots 179

Instant Pots & Multicookers 200

One-Bowl Cakes 225

No-Pots, Go-Withs & Basics 239

Introduction

**ROASTED CHICKEN "TAGINE"
WITH DATES, OLIVES, AND
LEMON, PAGE 24**

There's nothing that makes me appreciate the streamlined ease of a one-pan meal more than watching a professional chef at work.

The first time I stepped into a restaurant kitchen to observe the cooks, it was at a popular, cavernous restaurant called An American Place in New York City, where I had a college job as a coat checker. Sometimes, on a warmish night when coats were sparse but the dining room was crowded, I'd slip into the kitchen to take in the drama.

There was all of the exciting bustle and energy you'd imagine, but what riveted me most was the elaborate choreography the cooking entailed, completely different from anything I'd seen done at home.

To make one menu item, a chef might use three separate pans, two bowls, and an array of plastic squeeze bottles. There'd be a skillet for sautéing the salmon fillet, an oval sizzle platter to crisp the skin, another skillet to brown the accompanying sugar snap peas. In one bowl, pea shoots would be tossed with a couple of squirts from various squeeze bottles; in another, a sauce was reheated over a bain-marie.

Scurrying in the background were the dishwashers who cleaned up every greasy pan, dirty spatula, and sticky bottle. Without them easing the flow, the chefs would have sweat even more profusely than they already did.

The whole thing made me understand why many recipes in chefs' cookbooks were such a pain to make in my home kitchen. Chefs don't care about using every pot and pan in the house, because they don't have to think about having them pile up in the sink; they have dozens of pots and pans . . . and people to clean them.

I took this lesson with me when I became a food writer and started coauthoring cookbooks with celebrity chefs. Could I translate what they did in a professional kitchen using half a dozen pots, pans, and bowls into a recipe that would work just as well at home using one or two?

That was where my obsession with recipe streamlining began. And it continues to this day, now that I'm a food reporter and recipe columnist for *The New York Times*. My job is to create recipes home cooks want to add to their repertoire. And for every single recipe I develop, whether for a cookbook or for my Good Appetite column at the paper, I deconstruct the process. Is there a way I could make this recipe easier, faster, and tastier? And what's the minimum number of pots, pans, and dishes I need to dirty to get here? It's a discipline that has slowly solidified into a less-is-more philosophy—less work, less mess, more flavor.

This book of one-pan recipes is the culmination of it all.

The recipes are simple but not simplistic, with complex, layered flavors that you can achieve with minimal stress.

Along with reducing the number of pots and pans all the way down to one, I've also limited the number of utensils and bowls. It's not just for the sake of cleanup, it's also for convenience and flow while cooking. It's just easier to use the same bowl in which you mixed your vegetables to whip up the salad dressing, without having to stop and wash it in between.

I've applied this same spirit of paring down to techniques as well. Case in point: where I can get away with not browning every side of every piece of chicken for a stew or a braise, I don't. In the Cheater's Chicken and Dumplings on page 233, I brown only as many chicken pieces as can fit in one layer in the Instant Pot at once. This browning builds up enough *fond* (those umami-rich bits on the bottom of the pan) to flavor the sauce, without you having to stand over the splattering pan to sear each piece.

Shortcuts like this mean that the majority of the recipes in this book are weeknight friendly—the kinds of meals you can start thinking about at 6:00 p.m. and have on the table by 7:00 p.m. But they're also weekend delicious, out-of-the-ordinary dishes you'd be proud to serve to guests.

Even though I'm a thoroughly committed omnivore, almost half of the recipes in this book are meatless. And many of the ones that do contain meat use a lot less of it than others of their kind. Plus, for every dish in which it will work without diminishing the flavors, I've included a vegan variation. I've been eating less meat in this ecologically fragile moment, and these recipes reflect that shift.

Finally, a note on the number of servings in these recipes. For this book, the yield is necessarily dictated by the size of the pot or pan: the larger the vessel, the more people you can feed from it. Big, deep pots like Dutch ovens and soup pots can hold more servings than shallow sheet pans and skillets (depending on the recipe). Therefore, it follows that sheet pan recipes tend to feed only 2 to 4 people, whereas something cooked in a soup pot may feed 6 to 8.

Of course, if you're hankering for one of the sheet pan recipes—maybe the Roasted Chicken "Tagine" with Dates, Olives, and Lemon on page 24—but looking to feed more than 3 or 4, you can always break the one-pan rule, double the ingredient amounts, and cook it all on two sheet pans. (Isn't every rule made to be broken?) Just keep in mind that having two pans in the oven rather than one might delay browning, so you may have to add a few extra minutes to the cook time. Or you can try bumping up the heat by 25 degrees to encourage caramelization. Running the pans under the broiler at the end can brown things up, too. Just keep an eye on everything and make adjustments as you go.

The recipes here are guides, meant to be followed but only up to a point. After all, you know your tastes and preferences, and your kitchen and kitchen equipment, better than I do. Trust your senses, trust your gut, and don't be afraid to experiment. Even if you do occasionally get something wrong, most of the time you'll get it deliciously right.

And in either case, you won't have a pile of dishes in the sink when you're done.

Sheet Pans

Crispy Lemon Chicken

with Potatoes, Oregano, and Capers

SERVES 4

1 lemon

1¾ pounds Yukon Gold potatoes, peeled and thinly sliced

2½ teaspoons dried oregano, divided

1½ teaspoons kosher salt, divided, plus more to taste

¾ teaspoon freshly ground black pepper, divided

3 tablespoons extra-virgin olive oil, divided

2¼ to 2½ pounds bone-in, skin-on chicken drumsticks and thighs

3 fat garlic cloves, minced or finely grated

Pinch of crushed red pepper flakes

Torn fresh parsley, basil, or mint leaves, for serving

1 tablespoon capers, drained, for serving

SWAP IT OUT

If you'd rather use bone-in breasts, let the potatoes roast for 25 minutes, then add the chicken and roast for 20 to 25 minutes longer.

This lemony, herby dish might be my favorite way to cook chicken and potatoes in one pan. The potatoes get a head start in the oven while chicken drumsticks and thighs marinate, absorbing the flavors of lemon zest, garlic, oregano, and red pepper flakes. Then the pieces are plopped on top of the potatoes so their glorious fat renders while everything roasts and crisps. It all emerges glistening, golden, and richly flavored. I love this served alongside a spinach salad, but any tumble of leafy greens will work.

1. Heat the oven to 425°F and, if you like, line a rimmed sheet pan with parchment paper or a silicone liner (not essential but helpful for cleaning up). Grate the zest from the lemon into a large bowl and cut the naked lemon in half. Set aside.

2. On the prepared sheet pan, combine the potatoes, ½ teaspoon of the oregano, ½ teaspoon of the salt, and ¼ teaspoon of the black pepper; toss well to coat. Spread the potatoes out in a single layer. Squeeze one lemon half all over the potatoes and drizzle with 1 tablespoon of the oil. Roast the potatoes for 15 minutes.

3. While the potatoes are roasting, pat the chicken dry with paper towels and season all over with the remaining 1 teaspoon salt and ½ teaspoon black pepper. To the bowl with the lemon zest, stir in the garlic, the remaining 2 teaspoons oregano, and red pepper flakes. Add the chicken and toss, making sure it gets well coated with all the seasonings.

4. After the potatoes have roasted for 15 minutes, add the chicken to the pan, placing the pieces skin side up on top of the potatoes. Drizzle the chicken and potatoes with the remaining 2 tablespoons oil. Continue to roast until the chicken and potatoes are cooked through and everything is golden and crisped, 25 to 35 minutes longer.

5. Transfer the chicken and potatoes to a platter or serving plates and sprinkle with the torn herbs. Scrape the pan juices into a bowl, squeeze in the remaining lemon half, and stir in the capers. Drizzle a little of the sauce over the chicken and potatoes and serve the remaining sauce on the side.

Tarragon Chicken

with Caramelized Onions and Butternut Squash

SERVES 3 TO 4

1 pound **butternut squash,** cut into 1-inch cubes

1 teaspoon **honey**

3 tablespoons **extra-virgin olive oil,** divided, plus more for drizzling

Pinch of **crushed red pepper flakes**

1½ teaspoons **kosher salt,** plus more as needed

2 large **onions,** sliced (about 4 cups)

½ teaspoon **freshly ground black pepper,** plus more as needed

3 tablespoons chopped **fresh tarragon leaves** (or 1 teaspoon dried tarragon)

2 **garlic cloves,** finely grated or minced

2 pounds **bone-in, skin-on chicken drumsticks and thighs**

Sherry vinegar, to taste

SWAP IT OUT

Cubed sweet potatoes or turnips can stand in for the butternut squash. Or use regular potatoes, omitting the honey. And if you're not a tarragon fan, chives or marjoram work just as well.

Pairing chicken with tarragon and garlic is a classic that never gets old. Here, the licorice-y herb is used to marinate bone-in drumsticks and thighs, which are then roasted on the same pan as sliced onions and cubes of butternut squash. As the chicken cooks, the fat renders, coating the vegetables, while the fragrant steam rising from the onions flavors the bird. It's a succulent, easy, and very satisfying dinner. If you prefer white meat, substitute bone-in chicken breast halves, and start checking them after 20 minutes.

1. Heat the oven to 425°F. In a large bowl, toss the squash with the honey, 1 tablespoon of the oil, red pepper flakes, and a pinch of salt. Arrange the squash on one side of a rimmed sheet pan.

2. Spread out the onions on the other side of the sheet pan. Drizzle the onions and squash with a little oil and sprinkle with salt and black pepper, tossing to coat the vegetables. Roast for 15 minutes.

3. Meanwhile, in the same bowl you used for the squash (you don't need to wash it first), stir together the tarragon, garlic, remaining 2 tablespoons oil, 1½ teaspoons salt, and ½ teaspoon black pepper. Add the chicken and toss to coat.

4. After the onions and squash have roasted for 15 minutes, toss them well. Add the chicken to the pan, nestling the pieces in with the vegetables, and roast until the chicken is cooked through and the onions and squash are browned and tender, 30 to 40 minutes. If the chicken skin or onions aren't as brown as you'd like, run the pan under the broiler for 1 to 2 minutes.

5. Place the chicken on a platter. Drizzle the onions and squash with sherry vinegar and sprinkle with more salt and black pepper, if needed. Spoon the vegetables around the chicken and serve.

Roasted Chicken "Tagine"

with Dates, Olives, and Lemon

SERVES 4

3 tablespoons extra-virgin olive oil, divided, plus more for drizzling

2 teaspoons kosher salt, divided

1 teaspoon tomato paste

¾ teaspoon ground turmeric

¾ teaspoon sweet paprika

¾ teaspoon finely ground black pepper

½ teaspoon ground ginger

¼ teaspoon ground cinnamon

Large pinch of freshly grated nutmeg

3 pounds bone-in, skin-on chicken pieces (legs, thighs, breasts, or a combination)

½ pound carrots, halved lengthwise (or quartered if thick)

½ pound sweet potatoes, cut lengthwise into ¾-inch-thick wedges

1 lemon, quartered

½ cup (about 3 ounces) pitted dates, sliced

1 cup mixed olives (with or without pits)

½ cup torn fresh herbs (cilantro, mint, parsley, or a combination), for serving

This crisp-skinned roasted chicken has all the flavors of a North African tagine—the fragrant spices, the tangy lemon and olives, and the sweet, almost candied dates—but with the streamlined preparation of a sheet pan meal. Serve it with flatbread that you've warmed in the oven while the chicken is roasting, or with the Buttery No-Cook Couscous on page 246. You'll definitely want something to catch all those glorious golden juices.

1. Place a rack in the center of the oven and heat oven to 425°F.

2. In a large bowl, stir together 2 tablespoons of the oil, 1½ teaspoons of the salt, the tomato paste, turmeric, paprika, pepper, ginger, cinnamon, and nutmeg. Add the chicken pieces to the bowl and rub the paste all over them, including under the skin. Arrange the chicken on a rimmed sheet pan.

3. In the same bowl (you don't need to wash it first), toss together the carrots, sweet potatoes, remaining 1 tablespoon oil, and remaining ½ teaspoon salt. Arrange the vegetables on the sheet pan with the chicken. Add the lemon quarters to the pan. Roast for 20 minutes.

4. Remove the sheet pan from the oven, then scatter the dates and olives in an even layer around the chicken among the vegetables. Drizzle with a little more oil, then return to the oven and roast until the chicken is cooked through, another 10 to 15 minutes for the white meat, and 15 to 20 minutes for the dark meat.

5. To serve, transfer the chicken to a platter and spoon the vegetables, dates, and olives next to it. Squeeze with the roasted lemon and scatter with the herbs.

SWAP IT OUT

You can substitute whole cherry tomatoes and mushrooms for the carrots and/or sweet potatoes. Add enough to surround the chicken without crowding the pan.

Sheet Pan Thanksgiving

Roast Turkey Breast, Maple-Glazed
Sweet Potatoes, and Brussels Sprouts

SERVES 4

1 boneless turkey breast
(2 to 2½ pounds)

2 teaspoons kosher salt,
divided, plus more as needed

½ teaspoon freshly ground
black pepper

2 large garlic cloves, finely
grated

¼ cup mayonnaise

2½ tablespoons za'atar

1 pound sweet potatoes,
peeled and cut lengthwise
into 1-inch-thick wedges

4 tablespoons extra-virgin
olive oil, divided, plus more
as needed

1 tablespoon maple syrup

Pinch of crushed red pepper
flakes

1 pound brussels sprouts,
trimmed and halved
lengthwise

½ teaspoon cumin seeds

Fresh lemon juice, to taste

SWAP IT OUT

Sliced acorn or butternut
squash, cut 1 inch thick,
can stand in for the sweet
potatoes. Broccoli florets or
broccolini can replace the
brussels sprouts.

If you've ever had a craving for the flavors of Thanksgiving dinner in, say, the middle of February, this recipe is for you. The turkey breast, slathered in mayonnaise and fragrant za'atar (a Middle Eastern mix of dried herbs, sesame, and sumac), roasts up gorgeously moist and juicy while the sweet potatoes caramelize and the brussels sprouts turn crisp and brown. I like to serve this with a creamy za'atar sauce on the side, but if you're going full-on Thanksgiving, your favorite cranberry sauce might be a more apropos option.

1. Heat the oven to 400°F. If the turkey breast comes tied, untie it. Pat the meat dry with paper towels. Season the turkey all over with 1½ teaspoons of the salt and the black pepper, then rub all over with the garlic.

2. In a small bowl, stir together the mayonnaise and za'atar. Transfer 2 tablespoons of the za'atar mayo to a separate small bowl and brush that all over the turkey. Set the remaining za'atar mayo aside. Let the turkey sit at room temperature for 15 minutes while you prepare everything else.

3. In a large bowl, toss together sweet potatoes, 1 tablespoon of the oil, the maple syrup, ¼ teaspoon of the salt, and the red pepper flakes. Place turkey on a rimmed sheet pan and arrange the potatoes in a single layer around it. Roast for 20 minutes.

4. In the same bowl (no need to wash it), toss the brussels sprouts with 2 tablespoons of the oil, the cumin seeds, and the remaining ¼ teaspoon salt. Give the potatoes a toss after roasting for 20 minutes, and push the wedges to one side of the pan to make room for the brussels sprouts. Add the sprouts and continue to roast until the sprouts and potatoes are golden brown and a thermometer inserted in the thickest part of the turkey registers 145°F, 20 to 30 minutes longer (for a total turkey roasting time of 40 to 50 minutes). Allow the meat to rest for 10 minutes before slicing.

5. While the turkey is resting, whisk the remaining 1 tablespoon oil into the reserved za'atar mayo; taste and add a little more oil and salt, if needed. Season to taste with lemon juice. Serve the za'atar mayo alongside the turkey and vegetables.

Meatball Sub Sandwiches

on Garlic Bread

SERVES 2 TO 4

FOR THE MEATBALLS

⅓ cup panko bread crumbs

¼ cup grated Parmesan cheese

3 tablespoons chopped fresh parsley leaves and tender stems

2 garlic cloves, finely grated or minced

¾ teaspoon kosher salt

½ teaspoon dried oregano

¼ teaspoon freshly ground black pepper

Pinch of crushed red pepper flakes

1 pound ground beef or turkey, very cold

1 large egg, beaten

You might wonder why there are two meatball Parmesan recipes in this book (see Cheesy Meatball Parm with Spinach, page 66). But they are such different (and delicious) creatures, and since I couldn't choose, I offer them both. In this sandwich version, meatballs are broiled on a sheet pan alongside classic Italian garlic bread slathered with butter, parsley, and red pepper flakes. Mozzarella is added to the meatballs at the end to cover them in melty puddles, then the cheese-laden meatballs are stuffed into the garlic bread with a little marinara sauce for sweetness. Made from start to finish in under 45 minutes, it's one of the quickest meatball parm iterations out there, and I think one of the best.

1. Place an oven rack 4 inches from the broiler and heat the broiler to high.

2. Make the meatballs: In a large bowl, combine the bread crumbs, Parmesan, parsley, garlic, salt, oregano, black pepper, and red pepper flakes, and mix well. Add the meat and egg and combine with your hands until well mixed. Form into 24 meatballs, each about 1¼ inches in diameter. Place the meatballs on one side of a rimmed sheet pan and broil until golden and firm, 6 to 9 minutes (you don't need to turn them). Turn off the broiler and set the oven to 425°F.

1 crusty Italian bread, preferably semolina, about 12 inches long

4 tablespoons (½ stick) unsalted butter, melted

2 garlic cloves, minced or finely grated

2 tablespoons finely chopped fresh parsley or basil

1 tablespoon grated Parmesan cheese

Pinch of crushed red pepper flakes

4 ounces fresh mozzarella, torn or cut into small pieces (1 cup)

1 cup marinara sauce, homemade, page 67, or store-bought, for serving

3. While the meatballs are broiling, **prepare the sandwiches:** Use a serrated knife to cut the Italian loaf in half lengthwise, almost but not quite all the way through, and pull it open like a book. Place the bread, cut side up, on a piece of foil just large enough to fit the opened loaf. Put the bread and foil on the empty side of the sheet pan, next to the meatballs (the foil keeps the bread from absorbing the meatball juices and getting soggy). Bake for 3 minutes to toast the bread lightly.

4. In a small bowl, stir together the melted butter, garlic, parsley, Parmesan, and red pepper flakes. Remove the sheet pan from the oven and brush this butter-garlic mixture all over the top of the bread. Using a spatula, push the cooked meatballs close to each other so they're touching. Sprinkle the mozzarella on top of the meatballs and return the pan to the oven to bake for 5 to 7 more minutes, until the bread is crisp and the mozzarella is melted.

5. To assemble the meatball sub, place the cheesy meatballs on the garlic bread, spoon a little of the marinara sauce on top, and smush the sandwich shut. Cut into pieces and serve more marinara sauce on the side for dunking.

Garlicky Pork Chops

with Cauliflower and Pomegranate

½ tablespoon dark brown sugar

1 teaspoon kosher salt, plus more as needed

2 teaspoons cumin seeds, divided

½ teaspoon ground cumin

½ teaspoon freshly ground black pepper, plus more as needed

¼ teaspoon crushed red pepper flakes, or to taste

2 garlic cloves, finely grated or minced

2 bone-in pork chops, about 1½ inches thick (1¾ pounds total)

1 large head cauliflower (about 2 pounds), trimmed and cut into bite-size florets

2 tablespoons extra-virgin olive oil

Fresh cilantro, mint, or parsley leaves and tender stems, torn, for serving

2 tablespoons pomegranate seeds, for serving

Lemon wedges, for serving

A blast in a very hot oven is what gives this pork-and-veg dinner its caramelized appeal. Both the chops and the cauliflower get deeply bronzed at the edges but stay nice and juicy inside. Seasoned with cumin, garlic, and a spark of red pepper flakes and topped with sweet magenta pomegranate seeds, it's a gorgeous, full-flavored meal without a lot of effort on your part. It's just as good for company as it is for a cozy family dinner.

1. Heat the oven to 450°F. In a small bowl, mix together the brown sugar, salt, 1 teaspoon of the cumin seeds, the ground cumin, black pepper, red pepper flakes, and garlic until it resembles wet sand.

2. Smear the mixture all over the pork and let sit at room temperature while the cauliflower roasts, or in the refrigerator for up to 24 hours.

3. On a rimmed sheet pan, toss the cauliflower with the oil and a large pinch each of salt and black pepper. Spread the mixture out into one layer and roast for 15 minutes.

4. Sprinkle the remaining 1 teaspoon cumin seeds over the cauliflower and give the florets a stir. Add the pork to the same pan, nestling the chops in with the florets. Roast for 10 minutes. Flip the chops over and give the florets another stir. Continue roasting until the pork is cooked through and the cauliflower is browned and tender, 5 to 10 minutes longer.

5. Transfer the pork to a cutting board and slice the meat off the bones. Serve the pork and cauliflower sprinkled with the herbs and pomegranate seeds, with the lemon wedges on the side for squeezing.

SWAP IT OUT

Substitute bone-in, skin-on chicken thighs for the pork chops. Just add them with the cauliflower in Step 3.

Full English Breakfast

8 ounces (4 cups) white button or cremini mushrooms, halved or quartered if large

4 small plum tomatoes, halved lengthwise

2 tablespoons extra-virgin olive oil, plus more for drizzling

1 teaspoon Worcestershire sauce, plus more for serving

3 fresh thyme sprigs

Kosher salt and freshly ground black pepper, as needed

8 breakfast sausage links, either cooked or uncooked is fine, pricked all over with a fork

4 large eggs

Buttered toast, for serving

There's always a night when you want to have breakfast for dinner, and this is how to do it British-style. Drizzled with Worcestershire sauce, the roasted mushrooms and tomatoes become especially savory, while the eggs are cooked until crisp-edged and runny-yolked, right in the sausage drippings. This recipe is a riff on sheet pan bacon and eggs, developed by Genevieve Ko, my brilliant colleague at *The New York Times*. My version works best with pork sausages, which will release a flavorful slick of brawny fat. But other kinds of sausages—turkey, chicken, plant-based—will also work well. Serve this with plenty of buttered toast and, if you like, baked beans (most authentically, straight from a can).

1. Heat the oven to 450°F.

2. In a medium bowl, toss together the mushrooms, tomatoes, oil, Worcestershire sauce, thyme sprigs, and a pinch each of salt and pepper. Place the sausage links onto a rimmed sheet pan and spread the vegetables evenly around the sausages. Bake until browned and crisp, 15 to 20 minutes, tossing halfway through.

3. Take the pan out of the oven and use a spatula to push the vegetables and sausages to one side. Drizzle the empty side of the pan with a little oil, then crack in the eggs; season lightly with salt and pepper. Immediately return the pan to the oven and roast until the whites are just set and the yolks are still runny, 3 to 5 minutes longer. If you prefer medium or hard egg yolks, cook a minute more.

4. Using a spatula, separate the eggs. Slide them off the pan and onto plates right away to stop the yolks from solidifying. Discard the thyme sprigs and serve the sausages and vegetables with the eggs, drizzling with Worcestershire sauce and adding more salt and pepper, if you like. Serve with the buttered toast.

VEGETARIAN UPGRADE

Plant-based sausages work well here, and you can replace the Worcestershire with vegan Worcestershire, tamari, or coconut aminos.

Sausage Bake

with Crunchy Potatoes, Red Cabbage, and Caraway

SERVES 4

1 teaspoon caraway seeds

1 teaspoon coriander seeds

4 tablespoons extra-virgin olive oil, divided, plus more as needed

1 pound Yukon Gold or white potatoes, cut into 1-inch pieces

½ large head red cabbage (about ¾ pound), core removed, cut into 1-inch-thick wedges

¾ teaspoon kosher salt, plus more to taste

1 large red onion, thinly sliced

4 fresh thyme sprigs

4 fresh pork, turkey, chicken, or other sausages (about 1 pound)

1½ tablespoons Dijon mustard, plus more for serving

1 lemon

½ cup chopped fresh dill

Pairing sweet red cabbage and musky caraway seeds is a classic, and possibly the best use for caraway outside of rye bread. Here, the caraway-seasoned cabbage is roasted on a sheet pan next to crisp golden potatoes. Mustard-coated sausages are nestled alongside so that they can leak their savory, rich juices all over the vegetables. You can make this with all kinds of sausages—anything from spicy turkey to bratwurst to hot vegan Italian links will work, though if your sausages are very lean, you might want to drizzle everything with a bit more oil.

1. Heat the oven to 425°F. Using the flat side of a heavy chef's knife and a cutting board, or a mortar and pestle, lightly crack the caraway and coriander seeds.

2. Brush a rimmed sheet pan with 1 tablespoon of the oil and spread out the potatoes on one side of the pan. Arrange the cabbage wedges on the other side of the pan, overlapping slightly to fit.

3. Sprinkle the cabbage with the cracked caraway and coriander seeds and the salt. Scatter the onion slices in an even layer over everything. Drizzle the vegetables with the remaining 3 tablespoons oil. Tuck in the thyme sprigs. Roast for 30 minutes.

4. Meanwhile, using a pastry brush or your hands, coat the sausages all over with the mustard.

5. When the potatoes and cabbage have roasted for 30 minutes, remove the sheet pan from the oven and use tongs to flip the cabbage (but not the potatoes). Arrange the sausages on top of the cabbage and potatoes and return the pan to the oven.

6. Roast until the vegetables and sausages are browned, another 15 to 25 minutes depending on what kind of sausages you've got. The sausages are done when they are no longer pink inside and are browned on top.

7. Remove the pan from the oven and discard the thyme sprigs. Grate lemon zest over the sausages and vegetables and sprinkle with the dill. Cut the zested lemon into wedges. Serve the sausages and vegetables with more mustard and lemon wedges on the side.

SWAP IT OUT

You can use green cabbage in place of the red cabbage. And if you're not a fan of caraway, feel free to substitute cumin seeds.

Tahini Roasted Cod

with Asparagus and Thyme

SERVES 4

FOR THE TAHINI SAUCE

1 tablespoon fresh lemon juice, plus more for serving

1 fat garlic clove, minced or finely grated

½ teaspoon kosher salt

⅓ cup tahini

3 to 5 tablespoons ice water

FOR THE COD

1 pound asparagus, trimmed

6 scallions, thinly sliced (white and green parts separated)

3 fresh thyme sprigs

2 tablespoons extra-virgin olive oil, plus more for serving

Kosher salt and freshly ground black pepper

4 (6- to 8-ounce) boneless, skinless cod fillets

Sesame seeds (optional)

This speedy, verdant dish is perfect for springtime, when asparagus is at its best. You can use thick or thin stalks here. Thin ones end up softer and wonderfully browned at their tips while thicker ones stay crisp and bright green. Either way, it's a delicious dish that's light, pretty, and deeply flavorful.

1. Heat the oven to 425°F.

2. Make the tahini sauce: In a small bowl, whisk together the lemon juice, garlic, and salt and let sit for 1 minute to dissolve the salt. Add the tahini. Whisk in the ice water, 1 tablespoon at a time, until the sauce is smooth enough to drizzle.

3. Make the cod: On a rimmed sheet pan, toss the asparagus, scallion whites, and thyme with the oil until well coated. Season with salt and pepper.

4. Lightly season the cod with salt and pepper and nestle the fish onto the pan. Pour ¼ cup of the tahini sauce into a separate bowl and brush 1 tablespoon of that sauce on top of each fillet (reserve the rest of the tahini sauce for serving). Roast until the cod is opaque in the center and the asparagus is tender, 10 to 14 minutes.

5. Drizzle the reserved tahini sauce on top of the fish and asparagus. Serve topped with the scallion greens, a drizzle of oil, a little more lemon juice, and a sprinkling of sesame seeds, if you like.

SWAP IT OUT

This lovely dish works with pretty much any fish fillets—salmon, hake, mackerel. Choose the freshest and best-looking fish at the market, and watch it carefully, taking the pan out of the oven when the fish is just cooked through. Broccolini makes a fine substitute for asparagus here.

VEG IT UP

If you've got room on your sheet pan, you can add some halved cherry tomatoes. They'll get warm and juicy but keep their shape in the brief roasting time.

Miso-Glazed Salmon

with Roasted Sugar Snap Peas

SERVES 4

4 (6-ounce) skin-on salmon fillets, about 1 inch thick

Kosher salt and freshly ground black pepper

1½ tablespoons maple syrup, agave, or honey

1 tablespoon white or red miso

1 tablespoon fresh lime juice, plus lime wedges for serving

2 teaspoons soy sauce

1 teaspoon fish sauce (optional; you can use more soy sauce instead)

1 garlic clove, grated

1 pound sugar snap peas, trimmed

2 tablespoons extra-virgin olive oil

Pinch of crushed red pepper flakes

¼ cup coarsely chopped fresh cilantro, both leaves and tender stems

Sweet and savory miso-glazed fish is one of the easiest dinners out there, especially when you pair it with sugar snap peas, roasted until tender on the very same pan. Rice would be the obvious side dish here, but the Buttery No-Cook Couscous on page 246 works equally well and gets you there even faster.

1. Heat the oven to 400°F and, if you like, line a sheet pan with a silicone liner or parchment paper (helpful when it's time to clean up). Season salmon fillets with ½ teaspoon each of salt and black pepper and place them on a plate.

2. In a small bowl, whisk together the maple syrup, miso, lime juice, soy sauce, fish sauce (if using), and garlic. Pour the mixture on top of the salmon and gently massage the marinade all over the fish. Let the fish marinate at room temperature while you start the peas.

3. In a medium bowl, toss the sugar snap peas with the oil, red pepper flakes, and a big pinch each of salt and black pepper. Spread the peas on the sheet pan. Roast the peas for 5 minutes.

4. Toss the peas, then push them over to one side of the sheet pan so there's room for the salmon. Add the salmon to the pan, skin side down. Continue roasting until the salmon is cooked through and opaque on top and the sugar snap peas are crisp-tender, 10 to 12 minutes longer. Sprinkle with cilantro and serve with lime wedges for squeezing.

SWAP IT OUT

Green beans, broccolini, or cherry tomatoes can stand in for the sugar snap peas. Or try another kind of fish. Just look for pieces that are about 1 inch thick, or you may have to adjust the timing slightly.

VEGAN UPGRADE

This recipe works perfectly with tofu and it's even easier. Slice one (14-ounce) package of firm tofu into 1-inch-thick slabs. Pat dry with paper towels and season with salt and pepper. Arrange tofu on a sheet pan and pour marinade all over. Add the seasoned peas and roast for 20 to 25 minutes.

Crispy Sausage-Stuffed Mushrooms

with Broccolini and Cherry Tomatoes

SERVES 4

1 pound spicy or sweet Italian pork sausage, casings removed

¾ cup panko bread crumbs

½ cup grated Parmesan cheese, plus more as needed

¼ cup fresh parsley leaves and tender stems, finely chopped, plus more for garnish

1 tablespoon fresh thyme, oregano, or marjoram leaves (or a mix), finely chopped

¼ cup dry white wine

2 fat garlic cloves, finely grated or minced

Kosher salt and freshly ground black pepper

4 large portobello mushroom caps, at least 5 inches in diameter

5 tablespoons extra-virgin olive oil, divided, plus more as needed

1 bunch broccolini (6 ounces), ends trimmed

1 pint cherry tomatoes

Lemon wedges, for garnish

This savory crowd-pleaser of a recipe pushes stuffed mushrooms to the max. Mounding sausage meat, cheese, and bread crumbs onto saucer-sized portobello mushroom caps instead of the usual bite-size white buttons turns everyone's favorite hors d'oeuvre into a satisfying dinner. Roasted on a sheet pan along with broccolini and cherry tomatoes, it's hearty, meaty, and filled with colorful veggies.

1. Heat the oven to 375°F. In a mixing bowl, combine the sausage, bread crumbs, Parmesan, parsley, thyme, wine, garlic, a pinch of salt, and a grind or two of pepper. Mix until everything is well incorporated (your hands are the best tool here).

2. Place the portobello caps on a rimmed sheet pan, cavities facing up. Drizzle 3 tablespoons of the oil all over the mushrooms and season with salt and pepper. Using a spoon, stuff the oiled mushroom caps with the sausage mixture, mounding it in the center of the caps. Sprinkle the caps with a little more Parmesan and lightly drizzle with more oil.

3. In a medium bowl, toss the broccolini and tomatoes with the remaining 2 tablespoons oil, a pinch of salt, and a grind of pepper. Spread the veggies out on the sheet pan with the stuffed portobellos.

4. Bake until the sausage is cooked through (an instant-read thermometer should register 160°F) and the veggies are tender, 30 to 40 minutes. Serve hot or warm, garnished with more parsley and lemon wedges.

SWAP IT OUT

You can substitute green beans, brussels sprouts, or broccoli or cauliflower florets for the broccolini, and sliced bell peppers or red onions for the cherry tomatoes.

VEGAN UPGRADE

Substitute vegan sausage for the meat, and vegan Parmesan for the dairy-based cheese—or leave the cheese out altogether and add an extra garlic clove, a little more salt, and an extra tablespoon of olive oil instead.

Stuffed Portobellos

with Creamy, Lemony Chickpeas

SERVES 4

4 large **portobello mushroom caps**, at least 5 inches in diameter

Kosher salt and freshly ground black pepper

½ cup **extra-virgin olive oil**, plus more as needed

2 (15.5-ounce) cans **chickpeas**, drained and rinsed, divided

4 **garlic cloves**, finely grated or minced

¼ cup **tahini**

Juice of a lemon, plus more to taste

1 tablespoon **fresh thyme leaves**

4 teaspoons **ground or crushed sumac**

½ teaspoon **cumin seeds**

8 ounces trimmed **green beans, broccolini, or cherry tomatoes** (or use a combination)

Fresh cilantro leaves, for garnish

VEG IT UP

Plop these on top of a bed of spinach, arugula, or baby kale tossed with a little olive oil and lemon juice. If your mushrooms come with stems attached, slice them up, toss with a little olive oil and salt, and add them to the sheet pan along with the other veggies.

I adapted this recipe from the great Nigel Slater, and like much of his work, it's both stunningly original and intuitive in that the idea makes perfect sense. Hummus-stuffed mushrooms! I should have thought of that! But I did not, and I'm so glad he did. The portobellos, spread with the garlicky, lemony paste, become meaty and juicy in the oven, like slices of steak covered in rich, tangy sauce. More chickpeas are sprinkled on top, turning chewy-crisp as they roast. I've streamlined the technique and added some veggies to the pan, but otherwise left Nigel's deliciousness alone.

1. Heat the oven to 425°F. Score the inside of each mushroom cap with the tip of a knife and arrange, cavity side up, in a single layer on a rimmed sheet pan. Sprinkle the mushrooms with salt and pepper and drizzle generously with oil.

2. In a blender, combine 1 can of the chickpeas, the garlic, tahini, lemon juice, and a large pinch of salt and blend to form a paste. With the motor running, slowly drizzle in the ½ cup oil, scraping down the sides once or twice. Use a spatula to stir in the thyme and sumac. Taste and add more lemon juice or salt if you like. It should be bright and tangy.

3. Fill each mushroom with the creamy chickpea mixture. Cover with the remaining can of chickpeas, gently pressing them into the hummus so they stick, then sprinkle with the cumin seeds and more salt.

4. Add the vegetables to the pan and drizzle everything— vegetables and mushrooms—with more oil, tossing the vegetables to coat them. Bake until the mushrooms are tender when pierced with a fork, 30 to 35 minutes.

5. Garnish with the cilantro leaves and serve warm or at room temperature.

Baked Lemony Feta

with Tomatoes and Sweet Peppers

SERVES 4

1 lemon

1 teaspoon coriander seeds

2 large red, yellow, or orange bell peppers (or a combination), sliced ½ inch thick

1 pint cherry or grape tomatoes

1 small red onion, cut into 1-inch wedges

½ teaspoon kosher salt

¼ teaspoon crushed red pepper flakes

Freshly ground black pepper

4 tablespoons extra-virgin olive oil, divided, plus more for garnish

2 feta blocks (6 to 8 ounces each)

1 large fresh rosemary sprig

½ cup torn fresh basil leaves (or use mint or cilantro), for garnish

This is my take on the whole baked feta cheese trend. I prefer a pasta-less version that is intensely flavored with lemon, coriander seeds, and roasted onion. The tomatoes and peppers add loads of color and sweetness, and the salty feta mellows as it bakes underneath a gloss of olive oil. Serve this while the feta is still soft and melty, with some crusty bread to scoop it all up. This might be one of the easiest and prettiest dinners in this whole book, and it's definitely one of my favorites.

1. Heat the oven to 450°F.

2. Cut half of the lemon into thin slices or wedges. Save the other lemon half for serving.

3. Using a mortar and pestle or the flat side of a chef's knife and a cutting board, lightly crack the coriander seeds.

4. On a rimmed sheet pan, combine the peppers, tomatoes, onion, lemon slices, cracked coriander seeds, salt, red pepper flakes, and a pinch of black pepper. Drizzle with 3 tablespoons of the oil and toss until evenly coated. Nestle the feta blocks and rosemary sprig among the vegetables and lightly drizzle with the remaining 1 tablespoon oil. Roast until the vegetables are tender and crisp, and the feta is golden brown, 22 to 30 minutes.

5. Squeeze the reserved lemon half over everything and scatter the basil on top, then drizzle with more oil, if you like. Serve hot or warm.

SWAP IT OUT

Mix up the vegetables as you like here. Green beans, brussels sprouts, broccoli or cauliflower florets, broccolini, thick asparagus spears, or mushrooms can stand in for the tomatoes and/or the peppers.

Roasted Cauliflower and Potatoes

with Harissa, Yogurt, and Toasted Almonds

SERVES 2 OR 3

2 tablespoons harissa paste or sauce

1½ teaspoons fine sea salt, divided, plus more to taste

½ teaspoon freshly ground black pepper, plus more as needed

½ teaspoon ground cumin

5½ tablespoons extra-virgin olive oil, divided, plus more as needed

1 large head of cauliflower (about 2 pounds), trimmed and cut into bite-size pieces

1¼ pounds Yukon Gold potatoes, cut into 1-inch chunks

2 leeks, white and light green parts, halved lengthwise and thinly sliced into half moons

½ teaspoon finely grated lemon zest (from ½ lemon)

1 cup plain yogurt (if using Greek yogurt, thin it down with a little milk until pourable)

1 fat garlic clove

1 cup mixed soft fresh herbs, such as dill, parsley, mint, or cilantro, torn

½ cup coarsely chopped toasted, salted almonds

Lemon wedges, as needed

This is a meatless riff on one of my all-time favorite sheet pan dinners: a spicy harissa-slathered chicken loaded with lemony leeks, crispy potatoes, and a salty, garlicky yogurt topping. Here, roasted cauliflower stands in for the poultry, and almonds are tossed in for crunch. Added bonus: without the chicken, this lively, highly festive meal comes together in a flash.

1. Heat the oven to 450°F.

2. In a large bowl, whisk together the harissa, 1¼ teaspoons of the salt, pepper, cumin, and 4 tablespoons of the oil. Add the cauliflower and potatoes and toss to combine.

3. In a medium bowl, mix together the leeks, lemon zest, the remaining ¼ teaspoon salt, and the remaining 1½ tablespoons oil.

4. On a large rimmed sheet pan, arrange the cauliflower and potatoes in a single layer. Roast for 20 minutes. Stir the vegetables and scatter the leeks over them.

5. Reduce the oven temperature to 425°F. Continue to roast until the potatoes are cooked through and everything is golden and slightly crisped, 15 to 20 minutes longer.

6. While the veggies cook, place the yogurt in a small bowl. Grate or use a press to press the garlic into the yogurt and season with a pinch each of salt and pepper. Stir well.

7. Spoon the yogurt sauce over the vegetables on the sheet pan. Then scatter the herbs and almonds over everything. Drizzle with oil and a few squeezes from a lemon wedge or two and serve at once, with remaining lemon wedges on the side.

VEGAN UPGRADE

Use a nondairy yogurt instead of the regular yogurt. Nut-based varieties (cashew or almond) go nicely with the flavors here, but any kind you have is totally fine.

Caramelized Carrots

with Pancetta, Olives, and Crispy Parmesan

SERVES 3 OR 4

1½ pounds carrots, cut lengthwise into halves or quarters (to make long, thin carrot sticks)

6 tablespoons extra-virgin olive oil, divided

½ teaspoon kosher salt, plus more as needed

4 ounces pancetta or bacon, finely diced (⅛-inch cubes)

¾ teaspoon cumin, fennel, or coriander seeds

½ cup coarsely shredded (not ground) Parmesan cheese

⅓ cup olives (preferably Castelvetrano, but any good olives will work), pitted, crushed, and chopped

1 fat garlic clove, finely grated or minced

1½ tablespoons fresh lemon juice, plus more to taste

⅛ teaspoon crushed red pepper flakes, plus more to taste

¼ cup chopped fresh mint or basil, for serving

As much as I love the caramelized roasted carrots, my favorite part of this brawny dish just might be the Parmesan, which transforms in the oven into cracker-like shards with a cheesy appeal. The olives and pancetta lend rich and salty notes, which are perfectly balanced by the sweetness of the roasted carrots. Bacon and cheese notwithstanding, this makes for a relatively light meal. If you want to round it out, serve it with a fried egg or dollops of yogurt on top, maybe nestled into a bowl of brown rice, farro, or polenta.

1. Heat the oven to 425°F. On a rimmed sheet pan, toss the carrots with 2 tablespoons of the oil and the salt until coated. Arrange the carrots in a single layer on the pan and roast for 20 minutes.

2. Add the pancetta and cumin seeds to the carrots and gently mix to combine. Sprinkle the Parmesan on top and roast for another 15 to 20 minutes, until the carrots are tender, the pancetta is rendered, and the cheese is golden brown and crunchy.

3. While the carrots are in the oven, in a small bowl, whisk together the olives, garlic, lemon juice, red pepper flakes, and a large pinch of salt. Drizzle in the remaining 4 tablespoons oil, whisking well.

4. Spoon the olive dressing all over the roasted carrots while they're still hot and toss to combine. Taste and add more salt, red pepper flakes, or lemon juice, if needed. Scatter mint over the top before serving.

SWAP IT OUT

Cauliflower or broccoli florets, or brussels sprouts, can stand in for the carrots. Just reduce the initial roasting time in Step 1 to 10 minutes.

VEG IT UP

Turn this into a warm salad by serving it on a bed of hearty greens like spinach, arugula, or kale that's been tossed with a little olive oil, lemon juice, and a pinch of salt.

VEGETARIAN UPGRADE

Just skip the pancetta, no one will miss it!

Spiced Brussels Sprouts

with Paneer and Tangy Lime Dressing

FOR THE BRUSSELS SPROUTS AND PANEER

½ teaspoon coriander seeds

½ teaspoon cumin seeds

½ teaspoon fennel or caraway seeds

1 pound brussels sprouts, trimmed and halved (about 4 cups)

1 bunch scallions, thinly sliced (white and green parts separated)

2 to 3 tablespoons extra-virgin olive oil, plus more as needed

½ teaspoon kosher salt, plus more as needed

8 ounces (about 2 cups) paneer cheese, crumbled

¼ teaspoon smoked paprika

Large pinch of cayenne (optional)

¼ cup fresh cilantro or mint leaves and tender stems, torn

Lime wedges, for serving

One of my go-to side dish hacks is sprinkling crunchy, cracked whole spices onto a pan of vegetables before roasting. The spices toast in the oven, releasing their fragrance and flavor, which can be absorbed by the likes of the brussels sprouts, cherry tomatoes, or sweet potatoes sharing the pan. Adding paneer turns a side dish into a light and tasty meal, one that's easily filled in with a little yogurt and some flatbread served on the side.

1. Make the brussels sprouts and paneer: Heat the oven to 425°F. Using a mortar and pestle or the flat side of a chef's knife and a cutting board, crack the coriander, cumin, and fennel seeds.

2. Place the brussels sprouts and scallion whites on a rimmed sheet pan. Drizzle with 1 tablespoon of the oil to coat and sprinkle with the cracked spices and salt. Stir to combine everything, then spread in an even layer in the pan. Roast for 15 minutes, until golden brown.

1 large garlic clove, finely grated or minced

1½ tablespoons fresh lime juice, plus more to taste

½ teaspoon ground cumin, plus more to taste

Kosher salt and freshly ground black pepper

5 tablespoons extra-virgin olive oil

3. While the sprouts are roasting, **make the lime vinaigrette:** In a small bowl, combine the garlic, lime juice, cumin, and a big pinch each of salt and pepper. Slowly whisk in the oil. Taste and adjust the salt, cumin, and lime; it should be tangy.

4. Raise the oven temperature to 475°F and sprinkle the paneer over the brussels sprouts. Lightly drizzle with another 1 to 2 tablespoons oil and sprinkle with another pinch of salt, the paprika, and cayenne, if using. Toss the sprouts and paneer to combine. Roast until the cheese gets slightly brown and the sprouts are browned and tender, 9 to 12 minutes.

5. Remove from the oven and drizzle the lime vinaigrette on the paneer and sprouts right away (it will be absorbed immediately). Sprinkle the cilantro and scallion greens on top. Drizzle with a little more oil, if you like, and serve with lime wedges for squeezing.

SWAP IT OUT

This recipe will work with a bevy of different veggies. Try subbing in broccoli or cauliflower florets, cherry tomatoes, mushrooms, small cubes of butternut squash, turnips, or sweet potato, sliced fennel, or 1-inch-thick wedges of cabbage. Different vegetables might need more or less time in the oven. The key is to let them cook until they are about 10 minutes shy of being done, then adding the paneer. Ricotta salata and feta make good paneer substitutes, though you'll probably want to hold back on the salt since they're both a lot saltier.

VEGAN UPGRADE

Substitute a 12- to 14-ounce package of firm or extra-firm tofu, patted dry and sliced into ½-inch-thick slabs, for the paneer. Add the slabs to the pan along with the brussels sprouts in Step 2. The tofu won't brown, but it will soak up all the good flavors.

Glazed Tofu

with Sweet Potatoes and Silky Red Peppers

SERVES 3 OR 4

2 (14-ounce) packages firm tofu, each cut crosswise into three 1½-inch-thick slices

1 pound sweet potatoes, peeled and cut lengthwise into ½-inch-thick wedges

1 large red (or yellow or orange) bell pepper, sliced into ½-inch-thick strips

1 tablespoon finely chopped fresh sage

1 teaspoon paprika

½ teaspoon kosher salt, plus more as needed

⅛ teaspoon ground allspice

Pinch of cayenne

¼ cup plus 3 tablespoons extra-virgin olive oil, divided

¼ cup soy sauce or tamari

1½ tablespoons apple cider vinegar

1½ tablespoons honey

4 garlic cloves, finely grated or minced

1 tablespoon ground coriander

Freshly ground black pepper

2 large shallots, cut into ¼-inch wedges

½ cup chopped fresh cilantro leaves and tender stems, for serving

If there's someone in your life who swears tofu is always boring and bland, this is the dish to change their mind. Full of verve from a pungent soy sauce–honey marinade zipped up with fresh sage and spices, it's deeply flavored, thoroughly tender, and utterly compelling. The vegetables roasted alongside get very soft and caramelized, the sweet potatoes becoming velvety and the peppers, juicy and sweet as they brown. And if your family and friends are still not impressed with the tofu, this dish works beautifully with chicken (see Swap It Out).

1. Heat the oven to 400°F and, if you like, line a rimmed sheet pan with a silicone liner or parchment paper.

2. Arrange the tofu pieces, cut side down, on a clean kitchen towel or paper towels. Cover with another towel and place a cutting board on top. If your cutting board is lightweight, stack a few cans or a skillet on top to weight it down. Let the tofu drain for at least 10 minutes and up to 30 minutes.

3. In a large bowl, toss the sweet potatoes, bell pepper, sage, paprika, salt, allspice, and cayenne with 3 tablespoons of the oil. Arrange in a single layer on the sheet pan and cook until the potatoes and peppers begin to soften, 15 minutes.

4. Meanwhile, in a small bowl, whisk together the remaining ¼ cup oil, the soy sauce, vinegar, honey, garlic, and coriander. Remove the towels from the tofu and lightly season with salt and pepper. Place the tofu in the same bowl you used for the sweet potatoes and pour in three-quarters of the soy sauce mixture. (Reserve the remaining sauce for serving.) Toss gently to combine.

5. Remove the sheet pan from the oven, scatter the shallots onto the sweet potatoes and peppers, and toss to incorporate. Nestle the tofu amid the vegetables, making sure the tofu is surrounded by them but not on top of them (the tofu should touch the sheet pan). If you have extra soy marinade from the large bowl, spoon it on top of the tofu. Bake until the tofu and vegetables are browned, 35 to 40 minutes, tossing the vegetables halfway through.

6. To serve, drizzle the reserved soy mixture on the tofu and vegetables, and top with the cilantro.

SWAP IT OUT

This recipe works beautifully with boneless chicken thighs. Substitute 1½ pounds thighs for the tofu and add them to the bowl in Step 4 with the soy marinade. You can use boneless breasts, too, but don't add them to the pan until the potatoes and peppers have roasted for 25 minutes, then roast for another 20 to 25 minutes. Or use one block of tofu and a few pieces of chicken to please meat eaters and tofu eaters all on one pan.

Chile Crisp Tofu

with Blistered Kale

SERVES 2 OR 3

1 (14-ounce) package firm or extra-firm tofu, drained and patted dry

3 tablespoons chile crisp condiment, plus more for serving

3 tablespoons soy sauce

1 tablespoon balsamic vinegar

2 teaspoons rice vinegar

3 teaspoons toasted sesame oil, divided

1 teaspoon honey or agave syrup

3 garlic cloves: 1 finely grated, 2 thinly sliced

2 tablespoons chopped scallions

2 tablespoons chopped fresh cilantro

Kosher salt

1 pound (about 8 cups) curly or lacinato kale, stems removed

1 tablespoon neutral oil, such as sunflower, safflower, or grapeseed

Lemon or lime wedges, for serving

Spicy chile crisp condiment took the food world by storm a few years ago, eclipsing Sriracha for chile sauce dominance. The thing about chile crisp is that it combines spice with texture, with nubby bits of chile flakes, ginger, and garlic adding crunch as well as flavor. If you don't have any chile crisp on hand, you can substitute another Asian hot sauce, such as sambal oelek or Sriracha, spiked with 2 teaspoons grated fresh ginger. It won't be as crispy, but it will still taste great.

SWAP IT OUT

Swap cherry tomatoes, green beans, brussels sprout halves, mushrooms, sugar snap peas, broccoli florets, or broccolini for the kale. Just add them to the sheet pan at the same time as the tofu, and bake them together, tossing the vegetables after 10 minutes. You can leave the tofu in the oven for up to 25 minutes if the vegetables need a little more time to finish cooking.

1. Heat the oven to 450°F and, if you like, line a rimmed sheet pan with a silicone liner or parchment paper (not essential, but helpful for cleaning up). Slice the tofu crosswise into 8 (½-inch-thick) slabs. Pat them dry with paper towels and arrange in a single layer on a plate. Cover the tofu slabs with paper towels and set aside.

2. In a small bowl, whisk together the chile crisp, soy sauce, balsamic vinegar, rice vinegar, 2 teaspoons of the sesame oil, the honey, grated garlic (save the slices for later), scallions, and cilantro.

3. Remove the paper towels from the tofu and arrange the slabs on one side of the sheet pan, leaving room for the kale. Season the tops of the tofu slabs with salt, then brush generously with the chile crisp mixture; flip and repeat on the other side. If you have any extra chile crisp mixture, pour it over the tofu; try to mound the scallion and cilantro bits onto the tofu rather than on the pan, where they may burn. Bake the tofu for 10 minutes.

4. While the tofu is in the oven, tear the kale into large pieces and place into a large bowl. Add the neutral oil and the remaining 1 teaspoon sesame oil, the sliced garlic, and a big pinch of salt and toss to combine.

5. Pile the kale into a mound on the empty side of the sheet pan next to the tofu and bake for 5 minutes. Use tongs to toss the kale, then bake for another 5 minutes, until the kale is blistered and crisp (the tofu won't crisp or brown very much, but it will absorb all the good flavors). Serve the tofu and kale immediately, with lemon or lime wedges for squeezing, and more chile crisp, if you like.

Skillets

SPICY TURKEY
LARB, PAGE 70

SWAP IT OUT

You can use pretty much any quick-cooking vegetable in place of the snow peas. Asparagus, cherry tomatoes, shiitake mushrooms, bell peppers, thin green beans, broccolini, or zucchini would all work perfectly well. Just avoid dense roots like carrots, which take longer to cook, and leafy greens, which will exude too much liquid.

Creamy Peanut Chicken

with Charred Snow Peas

SERVES 4

½ cup creamy or crunchy natural peanut butter (preferably without added sugar)

1 tablespoon toasted sesame oil

1½ tablespoons rice vinegar, divided, plus more for serving

2 teaspoons light or dark brown sugar

2 teaspoons grated fresh ginger

2 garlic cloves, finely grated or minced

2 teaspoons soy sauce

1 teaspoon fish sauce

1 pound boneless, skinless chicken thighs or breasts, cut into 1-inch pieces

¾ teaspoon kosher salt, plus more to taste

3 tablespoons neutral oil, such as safflower, sunflower, or grapeseed, divided

1 bunch scallions, sliced (white and green parts separated)

5 cups (about 12 ounces) snow peas, trimmed

White rice, for serving

½ cup fresh basil, sliced, for serving

This dish has the same rich, creamy, and gingery notes of cold noodles with peanut sauce, except applied to a chicken and snow pea stir-fry, making it a bit lighter and full of protein. You can use either thigh meat or breast meat here. The thigh is more forgiving, providing a pretty wide margin of error. If you use the breast meat, just keep an eye on it, pulling it off the heat as soon as it's cooked through; overcooked chicken breast is always dry.

1. In a medium bowl, stir together the peanut butter, sesame oil, 1 tablespoon of the vinegar, the brown sugar, ginger, garlic, soy sauce, fish sauce, and enough water to reach a sauce-like consistency (anywhere from ¼ cup to ½ cup, depending on your peanut butter brand).

2. In a separate medium bowl, toss the chicken with the salt.

3. Heat a large skillet over high heat, then add 2 tablespoons of the neutral oil. Let the oil heat until it thins out, then carefully add the chicken and cook, stirring almost constantly, until the chicken is no longer pink and just cooked through, 3 to 5 minutes. Immediately transfer to a clean bowl.

4. Add the remaining 1 tablespoon neutral oil to the skillet, then stir in the scallion whites. Cook for 1 minute, then stir in the snow peas. Cook until charred, stirring occasionally, about 3 minutes.

5. Turn off the heat and stir in the remaining ½ tablespoon vinegar. Return the chicken to the skillet and add the peanut butter mixture. Toss to coat everything with the sauce. Taste and add a little more salt, if needed.

6. Serve immediately with rice, with basil and scallion greens on top, and with more vinegar on the side for drizzling.

Spiced Pork Chops

with Buttery Peas, Radishes, and Mint

SERVES 4

4 garlic cloves, minced or finely grated

2¼ teaspoons kosher salt, divided

2 teaspoons aromatic spice blend, such as baharat or garam masala

¼ teaspoon freshly ground black pepper, plus more to taste

4 (1¼-inch-thick) center-cut bone-in pork chops (about ¾ pound each)

3 tablespoons unsalted butter, divided

1 large shallot, thinly sliced

2 cups fresh or frozen peas (a 10-ounce package, no need to thaw them)

1 cup thinly sliced radishes

1 teaspoon grated lemon zest

¼ cup chopped fresh mint

¼ cup chopped fresh cilantro (or use more mint or parsley)

Flaky sea salt, for serving

With its combination of sweet, tender peas, radishes, and fresh mint, this dish seems like the essence of spring—except that you can make it all year round with frozen peas. The crispy pork chops, bathed in a sizzling spice butter and nestled among vegetables to soak up all the rich juices, make for a pretty substantial meal on their own, but if you want to round things out, try the Buttery No-Cook Couscous on page 246.

1. Heat the oven to 400°F.

2. In a small bowl, combine the garlic, 2 teaspoons of the kosher salt, the spice blend, and black pepper. Rub the mixture all over the pork chops and set aside while you prepare the other ingredients.

3. In a large ovenproof skillet, melt 2 tablespoons of the butter over medium-high heat. Add the pork and sear, without moving, until dark golden, 4 to 5 minutes per side. Transfer to a plate.

4. Reduce the heat to medium and add the remaining 1 tablespoon butter to the skillet, then stir in the shallot and cook until lightly golden, 2 to 3 minutes. Add the peas, radishes, remaining ¼ teaspoon kosher salt, and a little more pepper, stirring everything to coat with the pan juices. Stir in ¼ cup water, scraping up any browned bits from the bottom of the skillet.

5. Nestle the chops in with the peas and bake until the pork is cooked through, 10 to 15 minutes, or until a thermometer inserted in the thickest part of a chop registers 135°F.

6. Sprinkle with lemon zest, mint, cilantro, and flaky sea salt before serving.

SWAP IT OUT

You can substitute 3 pounds bone-in lamb chops for the pork. Season and brown them just the same. Roast in the oven for 7 to 12 minutes, until the thermometer reads 125°F for rare.

VEG IT UP

You can add another cup of peas to the pan to use a 16-ounce bag—the sauce can take it. Or add 2 to 3 ounces baby spinach to the pan after the shallot is tender in Step 4.

Cheesy Meatball Parm

with Spinach

SERVES 4 TO 6

FOR THE MEATBALLS

½ cup panko bread crumbs

¼ cup grated Parmesan cheese

¼ cup fresh parsley leaves and tender stems, finely chopped

2 garlic cloves, finely grated or minced

1 teaspoon kosher salt

¾ teaspoon dried oregano

½ teaspoon freshly ground black pepper

Pinch of crushed red pepper flakes (optional)

1½ pounds ground beef, turkey, pork, or chicken (or use a combination of ground meats), very cold

1 large egg, beaten

1 tablespoon extra-virgin olive oil, plus more as needed

Stirring fistfuls of spinach into this otherwise classic meatball parm adds a nice pop of color along with all those health-giving nutrients that make you feel better about eating a pan full of gooey melted cheese. If you're in a rush, you can shave 20 minutes off your time by using premade tomato sauce. And if you've bought two 1-pound packages of meat for this recipe, freeze the remaining half pound for the next time you want to make meatballs. It's fine to mix different kinds of ground meats together for this if that's what's in the freezer.

1. Make the meatballs: Heat the oven to 450°F. In a large bowl, combine the bread crumbs, Parmesan, parsley, garlic, salt, oregano, black pepper, and red pepper flakes, if using, and mix well. Add the meat and egg and combine with your hands until well mixed. If you have time, cover the mixture and chill it for 1 hour (or up to 24 hours). It's easier to form into balls while very cold (don't worry if you don't have time to chill the mixture first; the meatballs will be a little stickier to work with but will taste the same). Form into 28 meatballs, each about 1¼ inches in diameter.

2. Heat the oil in an ovenproof 12-inch skillet over medium-high heat. When the oil is hot, add enough of the meatballs to fit in one layer without crowding. Brown the meatballs on all sides, 6 to 10 minutes total (they do not need to be cooked through). Transfer to a plate, and repeat until all the meatballs are browned, adding more oil to the pan as needed.

3. Make everything else: When the meatballs are all browned, discard all but 2 tablespoons of the drippings in the skillet (if your meat was very lean, you might have to add a little more oil). Turn the heat to medium and add the garlic; cook, stirring frequently, until just lightly golden, 2 minutes. Add the red pepper flakes, if desired, and cook for 30 seconds. Stir in the tomatoes and juices (or the marinara sauce), basil, kosher salt, and black pepper.

Extra-virgin olive oil, as
needed

2 garlic cloves, thinly sliced

Pinch of crushed red pepper
flakes (optional)

1 (28-ounce) can whole or
diced plum tomatoes (or one
25- to 28-ounce jar marinara
sauce)

2 sprigs fresh basil or thyme
or 1 sprig fresh rosemary

½ teaspoon kosher salt, or
to taste

Pinch of freshly ground black
pepper

5 ounces (about 5 cups) baby
spinach, coarsely chopped,
divided

8 ounces fresh mozzarella,
torn or cut into small pieces
(about 2 cups)

¼ cup grated Parmesan
cheese

Flaky sea salt, as needed

4. Bring the sauce to a simmer, scraping up the browned bits on the bottom of the skillet. Cook until the sauce is thick and the tomatoes have mostly fallen apart, 20 to 25 minutes (or 5 minutes for the marinara sauce). Adjust the heat as needed to keep the sauce at a steady simmer. If using whole plum tomatoes, mash them up with the back of a wooden spoon or a potato masher to help them break down.

5. Discard the basil and stir in 4 cups of the spinach. Continue to cook, stirring occasionally, until the spinach wilts and the sauce thickens, 7 to 10 minutes longer. Return the meatballs and their juices to the pan. Gently toss the meatballs to cover with sauce. Sprinkle the mozzarella and Parmesan on top of the meatballs. Bake until the cheese is melted and browned in spots and the meatballs are cooked through, about 20 minutes.

6. To serve, top the meatballs with the remaining 1 cup spinach. Drizzle the spinach with a little oil and sprinkle with flaky sea salt.

Spicy Turkey Larb

with Soft Herbs and Lettuces

SERVES 4

3 tablespoons white rice (any kind is fine)

2 tablespoons coconut oil (or use peanut or grapeseed oil)

1 shallot, thinly sliced, plus more for serving

3 scallions, thinly sliced (white and green parts separated)

2 garlic cloves, finely grated or minced

¾ teaspoon kosher salt, plus more as needed

Large pinch of crushed red pepper flakes

1 pound ground turkey (or use chicken or pork)

2 tablespoons fresh lime juice, plus more to taste, plus lime wedges, for serving

1 tablespoon fish sauce or soy sauce, plus more to taste

1 cup fresh mixed soft herbs (such as cilantro, mint, and basil leaves or any combination), coarsely chopped, plus more for serving

1 fresh Thai, serrano, or jalapeño chile, seeded and thinly sliced

Large lettuce leaves, such as butter lettuce, romaine, or green leaf, for serving

Shredded carrots, for serving

Larb, a spicy, tangy meat salad from Thailand and Laos spiked with chiles, lime juice, and plenty of herbs, can be made from almost any chopped or ground protein—from pork to fish to tofu. This ground turkey version is a perfect midweek meal. The toasted rice powder is traditional and adds a layer of nutty flavor, but feel free to skip it if you're pressed for time. Rice or rice noodles would add some heft to your meal.

1. Put the rice in a large skillet set over medium-high heat, and let it toast, stirring frequently, until it starts to smell nutty and turns golden, 3 to 4 minutes. Pour the rice into a mortar and pestle or a clean spice grinder and allow to cool for 2 to 3 minutes. Pulverize to a coarse powder. Set aside.

2. Wipe out the skillet and return it to medium heat. Add the oil and let it heat. Add the shallot and scallion whites and cook until softened, 2 to 3 minutes. Add the garlic, salt, and red pepper flakes. Cook until fragrant, 30 to 60 seconds.

3. Stir in the turkey, raise the heat to high, and cook, breaking up the meat with a wooden spoon, until it's browned and cooked through, about 8 minutes. Using a flat spatula, press down on the turkey as it cooks so it can get a little crunchy on the bottom.

4. Add the lime juice and fish sauce to the pan and toss well with the meat and vegetables. Let cook for 1 minute, then remove the pan from the heat and stir in the herbs, chile, and toasted rice powder. Taste and add more lime juice if it needs brightness, or fish sauce if it needs a salty, umami depth.

5. Spoon the turkey onto a platter and serve with lettuce leaves on the side for wrapping, along with all of the garnishes—scallion greens, shallot, carrots, herbs, and lime wedges—for people to add to their lettuce rolls as desired.

VEGAN UPGRADE

Freeze one package of tofu for at least 6 hours, then thaw and drain. Wrap in a towel and press down. Crumble and use it in place of the meat.

Crispy, Spicy Lamb
with Greens and Avocado

SERVES 2 OR 3

1 tablespoon **extra-virgin olive oil**

1 large **onion**, diced

¾ teaspoon **kosher salt**, plus more as needed

1 **jalapeño**, seeded if you like, sliced

1 tablespoon grated **fresh ginger**

3 **garlic cloves**, grated or finely minced

2 teaspoons **garam masala**, plus more for serving

1 pound **ground lamb** (or beef or turkey)

½ teaspoon **freshly ground black pepper**

2 cups chopped **fresh tomatoes**

3 ounces (3 cups) **baby greens**, such as spinach, pea shoots, kale, or arugula

2 ripe **avocados**

Lime wedges, for serving

¼ cup torn **fresh cilantro leaves and tender stems**

This savory lamb sauté was inspired by keema, a traditional Indian dish of spiced ground meat simmered with onions, tomatoes, and sometimes peas. In this version, I add leafy greens, which wilt in the aromatic drippings and add color and verve to the richness of the meat. I like to serve it with soft slices of avocado on the side, and you can add some rice or flatbread to round it all out.

1. In a large skillet, heat the oil over medium-high heat. Add the onion and a large pinch of salt, and cook until it starts to brown, about 5 minutes. Stir in the jalapeño, ginger, and garlic, and cook for 1 minute.

2. Stir in the garam masala and cook until fragrant, about 20 seconds, then add the lamb, ¾ teaspoon salt, and the pepper. Use a spoon to break up the lamb as it cooks, stirring occasionally, until it is no longer pink, 3 to 5 minutes.

3. Add the tomatoes and cover the pan. Reduce the heat to medium-low and cook, stirring occasionally, until the tomatoes have softened, about 20 minutes. The mixture should look somewhat dry but not stick to the pan—if it does stick, add a splash of water. And if it looks too liquid-y, uncover, raise the heat, and let some moisture evaporate. Taste and add more salt, if necessary, then stir in the greens. Cook, uncovered, stirring occasionally, until the greens are just wilted, about 4 minutes.

4. Slice the avocados, squeeze a lime wedge or two over the slices, and sprinkle with salt and more garam masala.

5. To serve, mound the lamb onto a serving platter, top with cilantro, and surround it with avocado slices. Serve immediately.

VEG IT UP

You can double the greens here. Just add a little more salt and oil to make sure they are well seasoned. Peas are a nice addition and are traditional in a keema. Stir 1 cup of thawed frozen peas into the skillet along with the greens.

Green Shakshuka

with Avocado, Chile, and Feta

SERVES 4

3 tablespoons **extra-virgin olive oil**, plus more for drizzling

3 **garlic cloves**, thinly sliced

¼ teaspoon **ground coriander**

Large pinch of **crushed red pepper flakes**, plus more for serving

3 **leeks**, white and light green parts, halved lengthwise and thinly sliced into half moons

10 ounces **tender greens**, such as spinach, arugula, tatsoi, baby kale, or a combination

1 cup coarsely chopped **soft fresh herbs**, such as basil, parsley, cilantro, or a combination, plus more for serving

Kosher salt and freshly ground black pepper

¼ cup crumbled **feta**, plus more for serving

1 **lemon**

4 to 8 large **eggs**

Sliced **avocado**, for serving

We make a lot of shakshuka in our house, both red and green, for brunch and for dinner. This green version is milder and lighter than its tomato-based cousin, and is perfect for when you are looking for ways to increase your leafy vegetable consumption, or just want to try something new. The joy of shakshuka of any color is the soft egg yolk running all over the savory, lightly spiced vegetables. Here, crumbled feta adds a salty bite, and avocado slices, a velvety texture. Serve it with some crusty bread to sop up all the saucy goodness.

1. Heat the oven to 375°F.

2. In a large ovenproof skillet, heat the oil over medium-high heat. Add the garlic, coriander, and red pepper flakes and cook until the garlic just starts to turn golden at the edges, about 1 minute. Stir in the leeks and cook, stirring, until they soften, 5 to 7 minutes.

3. Stir in the greens, a handful at a time, and cook until almost wilted, 1 to 3 minutes. Toss in the herbs and season with a large pinch of salt. Once the greens are thoroughly wilted, another 1 to 2 minutes, stir in the feta. Grate 1 teaspoon lemon zest directly into the pan, then add a few tablespoons of water if the pan looks dry (the greens should be very moist). Cut the zested lemon into wedges and set aside.

4. Using the back of a spoon, create as many divots in the greens as you have eggs. Carefully crack an egg into each divot and season with salt and black pepper. Transfer the skillet to the oven and bake until the eggs are just opaque but still jiggly, 7 to 10 minutes.

5. Remove the skillet from the oven. Top the shakshuka with avocado slices, then drizzle with a little oil. Garnish generously with more feta, additional chopped herbs, red pepper flakes, and a squeeze of lemon. Serve with lemon wedges on the side.

Spicy Stir-Fried Pork

with Green Beans and Tomatoes

SERVES 3 OR 4

2 tablespoons neutral oil, such as peanut, sunflower, or grapeseed, plus more if needed

1 pound ground pork

1 teaspoon kosher salt, divided

8 ounces green beans, cut into ½-inch lengths

1 pint cherry or grape tomatoes, halved

1 to 2 jalapeño or serrano chiles, seeded if you like, thinly sliced

1 tablespoon grated fresh ginger

5 garlic cloves, minced

1 teaspoon cumin seeds

¼ cup chopped fresh cilantro leaves and tender stems, plus more for serving

3 tablespoons rice vinegar, plus more for serving

4 teaspoons soy sauce, plus more for serving

½ teaspoon sugar

In this light and summery meal, ground pork, green beans, and juicy, sweet tomatoes are stir-fried with plenty of ginger, garlic, and chiles, and seasoned with soy sauce and cilantro. A splash of rice vinegar, added at the end, gives a hit of acidity, which balances the richness of the pork. The whole thing comes together in less than 20 minutes. The most time-consuming part is browning the pork. But don't stint on this. The crispy mahogany nuggets of ground pork are my favorite part of the dish—crunchy and salty, almost like meaty popcorn. Also, all that brown matter stuck to the bottom of your pan is culinary gold, imbuing the sauce with flavor.

1. Heat a large skillet over medium-high heat for 1 minute, then add the oil and heat for another 30 seconds—it should be hot but not smoking. Stir in the pork and ¾ teaspoon salt, and cook, breaking up the meat with a spoon, until browned and crispy, 6 to 9 minutes. Use a slotted spoon to transfer the pork to a plate.

2. Return the pan to the heat and add more oil if it looks dry. Stir in the green beans and tomatoes and cook for 30 seconds. Stir in the chiles, ginger, garlic, cumin seeds, and remaining ¼ teaspoon salt. Cook, stirring frequently, until fragrant, about 1 more minute.

3. Return the pork to the skillet, along with the cilantro, vinegar, soy sauce, and sugar. Stir briefly to combine, then scrape onto a serving platter.

4. To serve, sprinkle with more vinegar and soy sauce to taste, then top with cilantro.

SWAP IT OUT

Ground turkey or chicken can stand in for the pork. Sliced green peppers or broccolini florets can replace the green beans.

VEGAN UPGRADE

Vegan ground meat will work here in place of pork, as will 8 ounces finely chopped shiitake mushrooms, added in Step 1. Just make sure to stir-fry the mushrooms until they're brown and crisp.

Seared Miso-Sesame Shrimp and Asparagus

SERVES 4

3 tablespoons white or yellow miso

2 tablespoons toasted sesame oil

1 tablespoon grated fresh ginger

2 teaspoons honey

Freshly ground black pepper

1½ pounds shrimp, peeled and deveined

2 tablespoons extra-virgin olive oil

1 pound asparagus, trimmed

Kosher salt

2 garlic cloves, finely grated or minced

Lime wedges, for serving

2 scallions, thinly sliced, for serving

Sesame seeds, for serving

This is one of those lightning-quick weeknight meals that you'll return to again and again. It's just so easy and so adaptable, with a pungent gingery sauce made from miso plus pantry staples that you can apply to almost anything (see Swap It Out). Here, sweet shrimp and juicy asparagus are stir-fried in the sauce until glazed and shiny, then topped with scallions for freshness, lime juice for a jolt of acid, and sesame seeds for crunch. Serve it as is for a light meal or round it out with a little rice.

1. In a large bowl, stir together the miso, sesame oil, ginger, honey, ¼ teaspoon pepper, and the shrimp. Let it sit while you prepare the asparagus.

2. In a 12-inch skillet, heat the olive oil over medium-high heat. Add the asparagus, sprinkle lightly with salt and generously with pepper, cover the pot, and cook, shaking the pan occasionally, until it is bright green but still firm, 3 to 4 minutes. Transfer the asparagus to a serving platter.

3. Add the shrimp and its marinade to the pan and cook until the shrimp is pink and tails curl in, about 5 minutes, flipping halfway through. Stir in the garlic and more pepper during the last minute, letting it become fragrant, then squeeze a lime wedge over the top. Taste and add a little salt, if needed.

4. Transfer the shrimp to the platter with the asparagus and toss well. Serve topped with scallions and sesame seeds, with more lime wedges on the side.

SWAP IT OUT

This technique can be used on so many different protein-and-vegetable combinations. Try strips of chicken breast, pork, or beef, or salmon fillets instead of shrimp. And broccoli or broccolini, sliced bell peppers, or sugar snap peas; mushrooms or chunks of cucumber can replace the asparagus.

Crispy Thai Omelet (Kai Jeow)

with Stir-Fried Cabbage and Herbs

SERVES 2

FOR THE CABBAGE

1 tablespoon neutral oil, such as grapeseed, sunflower, or safflower

4 garlic cloves, thinly sliced

3 cups thinly sliced green cabbage (from about ½ small head)

1 teaspoon fish sauce, plus more to taste

½ teaspoon freshly ground white or black pepper

FOR THE OMELET

2 tablespoons plus 2 teaspoons fish sauce, divided

1 teaspoon fresh lime juice, plus more to taste

1 teaspoon light brown sugar

3 scallions, thinly sliced, divided

1 small red or green chile, seeded if you like, thinly sliced, divided

4 large eggs

2 tablespoons neutral oil, such as grapeseed, sunflower, or safflower

1 cup torn fresh basil or cilantro leaves, or a combination

Thin, crisp-edged, laced with herbs and chile, and seasoned with pungent fish sauce, Thai omelets are completely different from the mild and fluffy French versions I grew up eating, and I absolutely adore them. Here, I pair one with soft sautéed cabbage, which adds a sweet note to the plate. Served as is, it makes for a somewhat light meal, but you can add some rice (the traditional kai jeow accompaniment) to make it more substantial.

1. Cook the cabbage: Heat a large nonstick or well-seasoned cast-iron skillet over high heat. Add the oil and garlic at the same time and cook for a few seconds, just until the garlic turns golden at the edges. Add the cabbage and sauté, tossing it well with the garlic, until it wilts and browns at the edges, 5 to 7 minutes. Add the fish sauce and ground pepper, tossing well. Taste and add more fish sauce, if needed. Transfer to a plate and wipe out the skillet.

2. Make the omelet: In a small bowl, combine 2 tablespoons of the fish sauce, the lime juice, brown sugar, half the scallions, and half the chile slices. Mix well to dissolve the sugar and set aside.

3. In a small bowl, whisk the eggs and the remaining 2 teaspoons fish sauce until smooth and frothy. Stir in the remaining scallions and chile slices.

4. In the same skillet you used for the cabbage, heat the oil over medium-high heat. You want the oil really hot, almost smoking. Carefully pour the egg mixture evenly across the skillet. Let the eggs cook, undisturbed, until they are golden brown underneath, 30 seconds to 1 minute. Using tongs or a wide spatula (or both, wielding one in each hand), carefully turn the omelet over, gently lowering it away from you. Cook until golden brown on the other side, about 1 minute. Transfer to a paper towel–lined plate.

5. Serve the omelet topped with the cabbage and the herbs, with the sauce alongside for dipping.

VEGETARIAN
UPGRADE

Skip the fish sauce and
use soy sauce, tamari, or
coconut aminos instead.
It makes for a slightly
less funky omelet, but
just as flavorful.

Parmesan White Beans and Kale

with Crunchy, Garlicky Bread Crumbs

FOR THE TOPPING

1 cup panko bread crumbs

2 tablespoons extra-virgin olive oil

2 tablespoons grated Parmesan cheese

1 garlic clove, finely grated, passed through a press or mashed to a paste

1 teaspoon fresh rosemary, finely chopped

Pinch of crushed red pepper flakes

Kosher salt and freshly ground black pepper

FOR THE BEANS

½ cup extra-virgin olive oil, plus more for serving

6 garlic cloves, thinly sliced

3 shallots, thinly sliced

1 pound (about 9 cups) kale, stems removed, coarsely chopped

¾ teaspoon kosher salt, plus more as needed

¼ teaspoon crushed red pepper flakes, plus more as needed

3 (15.5-ounce) cans white beans (such as cannellini), drained and rinsed

1 cup vegetable or chicken stock

⅔ cup grated Parmesan cheese, plus more for serving

Lemon wedges or balsamic vinegar, for serving

In this hearty meatless meal, canned white beans, sautéed shallots, and loads of kale are stewed in a Parmesan-flavored broth, then topped with a shaggy, crispy bread crumb topping. To make this easy meal even simpler, skip the topping, and serve bowls of the beans accompanied by garlicky crostini—that is, toasted country bread rubbed with cut garlic slices and drizzled with olive oil. And if you pull out your best olive oil for drizzling on at the end, you won't regret it. It makes a difference.

1. Heat the oven to 425°F.

2. Prepare the topping: In a medium bowl, combine the bread crumbs, oil, Parmesan, garlic, rosemary, and red pepper flakes. Season with salt and black pepper. Set aside.

3. Make the beans: In a large ovenproof skillet or sauté pan, combine the oil, sliced garlic, and shallots and place the pan over medium-high heat. Cook until the garlic and shallots are golden in spots, 4 to 6 minutes. Stir in the kale, salt, and red pepper flakes and cook until the kale is wilted and almost tender, 5 to 10 minutes. If the pan dries out, add a splash of water.

4. Stir in the beans and stock and bring the mixture to a gentle simmer. Cover and cook until the kale is very tender and some but not all of the stock has evaporated, about 5 minutes (it should be on the soupy side).

5. Stir in the Parmesan, then taste and add more salt, if needed. Spread the beans and kale in an even layer in the skillet and sprinkle with the reserved topping. Bake until the bread crumbs are golden brown, about 12 minutes. If you'd like more color on your bread crumb topping, broil for a minute or two (watch carefully so it doesn't burn).

6. To serve, top with more Parmesan, a drizzle of oil, a squeeze of lemon or drizzle of balsamic vinegar, and red pepper flakes, if you'd like.

VEG IT UP

You can add 1 cup of halved cherry tomatoes seasoned with a little salt to the pan along with the beans. Or, add a sliced bell pepper to the pan along with the shallots and increase the cooking time to make sure everything is thoroughly soft before adding the kale (probably another 5 to 7 minutes). Or do both.

VEGAN UPGRADE

Skip the Parmesan and, for the topping, increase the panko to 1½ cups and add another 2 tablespoons oil to the crumbs.

Farro with Spicy Sausage and Apple Cider

6 tablespoons extra-virgin olive oil, divided, plus more for drizzling

12 ounces spicy Italian sausage (pork, turkey, or chicken), removed from the casings

1 large red onion, halved and thinly sliced into half moons

1 cup apple cider

2 fresh rosemary sprigs

1 teaspoon kosher salt, plus more to taste

1½ cups pearled or semi-pearled farro

1 cup chopped fresh parsley leaves and tender stems, plus more for garnish

1 cup torn fresh mint leaves and tender stems, plus more for garnish

½ cup grated Parmesan cheese (about 2 ounces), plus more for garnish

2 teaspoons apple cider vinegar, or to taste

2 cups arugula leaves

Flaky sea salt, for serving

A few years ago, I published a summery farro salad recipe based on one served at New York City's Charlie Bird restaurant. Enriched with olive oil and Parmesan, sweetened with apple cider, and made juicy and bright from cherry tomatoes and loads of fresh herbs, it was so popular that even the great Ina Garten was a fan. Here, I've turned those same flavors (minus the tomatoes)—augmented with nuggets of Italian pork sausage—into a cozy, wintry skillet dinner. It's more substantial than the salad but just as appealing.

1. In a 10-inch sauté pan or large skillet, heat 2 tablespoons of the oil over medium-high heat. Add the sausage and about three-quarters of the onion slices (save the remaining onion for later), and cook, stirring occasionally, until the onion is tender and the sausage is browned in spots, 7 to 10 minutes.

2. Add the apple cider, rosemary, kosher salt, and 2 cups water to the pan and bring to a simmer, scraping up the browned bits on the bottom of the pan. Stir in the farro. When the liquid returns to a simmer, lower the heat to medium-low and cover the pan. Cook until the liquid evaporates and the farro is tender, 25 to 35 minutes (pearled farro cooks more quickly than semi-pearled). If the pan dries out during cooking, add a little more water.

3. Discard the rosemary sprigs. Stir in the reserved onion, the parsley, mint, Parmesan, vinegar, and remaining 4 tablespoons oil. Taste, and add more salt and vinegar, if needed.

4. Just before serving, top the farro with the arugula and more parsley and mint, drizzle with a little more oil, and sprinkle with flaky sea salt and more Parmesan, if you like.

SWAP IT OUT

If you don't have apple cider, you can use water or stock as a substitute. The final dish will lack the sweetness of the cider and, if you like, you can stir in a little honey or maple syrup at the end to make up for it.

VEGAN UPGRADE

You can use vegan sausage here, and substitute ¼ cup nutritional yeast for the Parmesan.

Farro with Crispy Spiced Chickpeas

Tomatoes and Leeks

SERVES 4 TO 6

2 (15.5-ounce) cans chickpeas, drained and rinsed

9 tablespoons extra-virgin olive oil, divided, plus more for drizzling

2½ teaspoons kosher salt, divided, plus more to taste

Freshly ground black pepper

4 tablespoons (½ stick) unsalted butter

1 teaspoon fennel seeds

½ teaspoon crushed red pepper flakes

2 tablespoons plus 2 teaspoons fresh lemon juice, divided, plus more to taste

2 leeks, white and light green parts, halved lengthwise and thinly sliced into half moons

2 cups diced fennel

3 fresh thyme sprigs

1½ cups pearled or semi-pearled farro

1 pint cherry tomatoes, halved

1 cup chopped fresh parsley, plus more for garnish

1 cup chopped fresh cilantro, plus more for garnish

1 garlic clove, finely grated or minced

1 teaspoon grated lemon zest

Flaky sea salt, for serving

Spiced crispy chickpeas are the glory of this homey, hardy, meatless dish, with loads of vegetables—soft sautéed fennel, cherry tomatoes, leeks, and 2 cups' worth of herbs—adding sweet freshness to the mix. Walking the line between a pilaf and a warm grain salad, it makes a satisfying meal on its own or will feed a crowd as a side dish to accompany roast chicken, fish, or grilled sausages.

1. Using a clean kitchen towel or paper towels, dry the drained chickpeas thoroughly. In a large skillet, heat 3 tablespoons of the oil over medium-high heat. Add the chickpeas, ½ teaspoon of the kosher salt, and a grind or two of black pepper to the skillet and cook, stirring occasionally, until crisped, 10 to 12 minutes. Add the butter, fennel seeds, and red pepper flakes, and cook until golden and nutty smelling, 1 to 2 minutes longer. Remove the pan from the heat and stir in 2 tablespoons of the lemon juice. Transfer the chickpeas to a plate and season with kosher salt and black pepper. Wipe out the skillet with paper towels.

2. Return the skillet to medium-high heat and add 3 tablespoons of the oil. Add the leeks, fennel, and a pinch each of kosher salt and black pepper, and cook, stirring occasionally, until tender and browned, 7 minutes.

3. Add 3 cups water, the thyme, and the remaining 2 teaspoons kosher salt and bring to a simmer, scraping up the browned bits on the bottom of the pan. Stir in the farro. When the liquid returns to a simmer, lower the heat to medium-low and cover the pan. Cook until the liquid evaporates and the farro is tender, 25 to 35 minutes (pearled farro cooks more quickly than semi-pearled). If the pan dries out during cooking, add a little more water.

4. Discard the thyme sprigs. Stir in the tomatoes, parsley, cilantro, garlic, lemon zest, and the remaining 2 teaspoons lemon juice and 3 tablespoons oil. Taste and add more kosher salt and lemon juice, if needed.

5. Just before serving, stir in the crispy chickpeas and more parsley and cilantro, drizzle with a little more oil, and sprinkle with flaky sea salt.

VEGAN UPGRADE

Skip the butter in Step 1, adding a little more olive oil instead. Or use cultured vegan butter.

Eggplant Rice Pilaf

with Feta, Lemon, and Mint

SERVES 3 OR 4

1½ cups long-grain white rice

¼ cup extra-virgin olive oil, plus more for drizzling

1 pound eggplant, cut into ½-inch cubes (about 6 cups)

1 teaspoon kosher salt, plus more as needed

1 small onion, diced

2 garlic cloves, minced

½ cinnamon stick (about 1½ inches) (optional)

1 bay leaf

1 tablespoon unsalted butter

2½ cups chicken or vegetable stock

1 lemon

½ cup (2 ounces) crumbled feta

½ cup torn fresh mint leaves (or use cilantro or basil)

Plain yogurt, for serving (optional)

Studded with golden cubes of eggplant, this delightful rice pilaf has a salty depth from crumbled feta, and a tart freshness from the combination of lemon and mint. The optional cinnamon stick lends an earthy, spicy note, but you can leave it out for something a little brighter. Serve this topped with yogurt for a light, meatless meal, or as a side dish to roasted meats, fish, or more roasted veggies.

1. Heat the oven to 350°F with a rack in the middle. Put the rice in a sieve and rinse under cool water until the water runs clear. Set aside.

2. Heat a 12-inch ovenproof skillet (if you have nonstick, use it!) with a tight-fitting lid over medium heat. Once it's hot, add the oil and let it heat up until it thins out. Add the eggplant in a single layer, cover the pan, and cook, stirring occasionally, until the eggplant is evenly browned and starts to stick, about 5 minutes. Use a slotted spoon to transfer the eggplant to a paper towel–lined plate and sprinkle lightly with salt.

3. Drizzle a little more oil into the pan and stir in the onion. Cook until softened, about 5 minutes (reduce the heat if the onion browns too quickly). Stir in the garlic, cinnamon stick (if using), bay leaf, and butter, and cook an additional 1 minute.

4. Stir in the rice and 1 teaspoon salt, and cook, stirring frequently, until it smells toasty, about 4 minutes. Add the stock and eggplant and bring to a simmer. Cover the pan and transfer to the oven.

5. Cook until the rice is cooked through, about 30 minutes.

6. Meanwhile, grate the zest from the lemon and cut the naked fruit into wedges. When the rice is done, remove the pan from the oven and fold in the feta and lemon zest with a fork, fluffing the rice as you go. Wrap the skillet cover in a clean kitchen towel to absorb the steam, then cover the skillet and let the pilaf sit for 10 minutes.

7. Remove the cinnamon stick and bay leaf. Stir in the mint, squeeze some lemon juice from the wedges over the rice, and drizzle with oil. Serve hot or warm, with a dollop of yogurt on the side, if you like.

VEG IT UP

Juicy diced tomatoes are excellent here. Season about 1 cup of them with salt and a little cayenne and stir them into the rice just before serving.

VEGAN UPGRADE

Sliced or slivered almonds make a terrific substitute for the feta cheese. You can toast them in a dry skillet for a few minutes, if you like, or sprinkle them on the rice untoasted. Either way, they add protein, crunch, and a mild, sweet flavor. If you want to take this in a brinier direction, swap in ½ cup chopped olives. Or use both!

Crispy Kimchi Fried Rice

with Scrambled Eggs and Scallions

SERVES 4 TO 6

4 tablespoons neutral oil, such as grapeseed, sunflower, or safflower, divided, plus more as needed

1 tablespoon toasted sesame oil, plus more for drizzling

1 small bunch scallions, sliced (white and green parts separated)

4 cups thinly sliced or shredded napa or green cabbage (from about ½ small head)

½ cup shredded carrots (from 2 to 3 carrots)

Kosher salt

4 garlic cloves, minced

1 tablespoon minced fresh ginger

6 cups cooked white or brown rice, preferably day-old short-grain rice

3 tablespoons fish sauce, plus more as needed

1 tablespoon soy sauce, plus more as needed

½ cup kimchi, drained and chopped, plus more for serving (optional)

½ cup green peas or shelled cooked edamame (thawed if frozen)

4 large eggs, beaten

The secret to getting truly crackling fried rice is to take the frying part seriously. Let the rice sizzle in the hot oil without moving it around too much. Using leftover rice also helps because it's drier than freshly cooked rice and therefore crisps more easily. But if you're starting from scratch, just cook up 2 cups of raw rice (see page 248), then spread it out on a sheet pan and let it cool and dehydrate a bit before frying. Here the rice is seasoned with kimchi for a spicy kick (which was inspired by bokkeumbap) and mixed with sweet cabbage and fluffy scrambled eggs. Be sure to have everything prepped and near the stove before you start; the cooking goes fast.

1. In a large nonstick skillet, heat 1 tablespoon of the neutral oil with the sesame oil over medium-high heat until almost smoking. Stir in the scallion whites. Cook until soft, stirring frequently, 1 to 2 minutes. If the pan looks dry, drizzle in a little more neutral oil, then stir in the cabbage, carrots, and a pinch of salt. Cook, continuing to stir frequently, until the cabbage is soft, 3 to 6 minutes. Stir in the garlic and ginger, and cook until fragrant, another 1 to 2 minutes. Transfer to a bowl.

2. Add the remaining 3 tablespoons neutral oil to the skillet and raise the heat to high. Add the rice and a large pinch of salt, then toss thoroughly to coat. Spread out the rice in an even layer in the bottom of the pan and drizzle with fish sauce and soy sauce. Let the rice sit until the sizzling stops and it starts to crackle and crisp, 1 to 4 minutes. Toss, taste, and add more fish sauce or soy sauce, if necessary. Fold in the cabbage mixture, kimchi, and peas, then transfer to plates.

3. If the pan looks dry, add a drizzle of neutral oil, let it heat for a few seconds, then pour in the beaten eggs, half the scallion greens, and a pinch of salt. Use a spatula to scramble the eggs until just set, 1 to 2 minutes. Top the rice with the eggs, the remaining scallion greens, and more kimchi, if you like (or serve more kimchi on the side). Drizzle everything with sesame oil and soy sauce and serve immediately.

VEG IT UP

If you want to add more veggies here, I'd suggest just increasing what's already going into the pan and using less rice. Substitute another 2 cups of cabbage or 1 cup of shredded carrots for 1 cup of cooked rice. Then taste and add more soy sauce and fish sauce, as needed. You can also double the peas.

VEGAN UPGRADE

Substitute coconut aminos or more soy sauce for the fish sauce, and skip the eggs. This dish is just as good without them.

Fried Chickpeas and Scrambled Eggs

with Garlicky Greens and Spicy Yogurt

SERVES 4

2 (15-ounce) cans chickpeas, drained and rinsed

2 teaspoons coriander seeds

2 teaspoons cumin seeds

2 teaspoons flaky sea salt

½ teaspoon crushed red pepper flakes

1 cup plain Greek yogurt

3 garlic cloves: 1 minced or finely grated, 2 thinly sliced

Kosher salt and freshly ground black pepper

4 tablespoons extra-virgin olive oil, divided

6 large eggs, beaten

6 scallions, thinly sliced

5 ounces (5 cups) baby kale or spinach, coarsely chopped

½ cup fresh cilantro leaves and tender stems, torn

Lime wedges, for serving

SWAP IT OUT

Feel free to change up the spices, substituting other whole seeds—caraway, fennel, sesame, mustard—for the cumin and coriander.

While I'd happily eat a plate of crunchy, salty fried chickpeas all by itself for dinner, the rest of my family needs a little more substance on the plate. Enter this super speedy meatless dish. After the chickpeas are fried with cracked coriander and cumin until golden and crisp, the skillet is given over to a soft egg scramble shot through with wilted greens, garlic, and scallions. To serve, the eggs are drizzled with a simple creamy yogurt sauce, then topped with the chickpeas, cilantro, and more of the salted cracked-spice mix. It makes a deeply piquant meal, with minimal effort.

1. Dry the drained chickpeas thoroughly with a clean kitchen towel or paper towels and set aside.

2. Using a mortar and pestle or the flat side of a chef's knife and a cutting board, crack the coriander and cumin seeds. In a small bowl, combine the spices with the flaky sea salt and red pepper flakes and set aside. In another small bowl, make the yogurt sauce: Whisk together the yogurt, the minced garlic, and a pinch of kosher salt and set aside for serving.

3. In a large skillet, heat 2 tablespoons of the oil over medium-high heat. Add the chickpeas and a pinch of kosher salt and cook, stirring occasionally, until crisped, 6 to 8 minutes. Stir in half of the spice mixture (save the rest for serving) and cook for another minute or two, until the spices are fragrant and toasted. Immediately transfer the chickpeas to a paper towel–lined plate.

4. Season the beaten eggs with a pinch of kosher salt and a grind of black pepper. In the same skillet used for the chickpeas (no need to wash it first), heat the remaining 2 tablespoons oil over medium-high heat and add the scallions and the thinly sliced garlic. Cook until golden at the edges, 1 to 2 minutes. Stir in the kale and a pinch of kosher salt, and cook until wilted, 1 to 2 minutes. Carefully pour in the eggs and cook, stirring frequently, until just set, 1 minute.

5. To serve, spoon eggs onto a dish, drizzle with yogurt sauce, and top with the chickpeas, cilantro, and more of the spice mixture. Squeeze a lime wedge on top and serve immediately.

Crunchy Peanut-Crusted Tofu

with Asparagus

SERVES 4

2 (14-ounce) packages firm tofu, each cut in half crosswise into 2 (1-inch-thick) blocks

Kosher salt and freshly ground black pepper

2 tablespoons sambal oelek or another Asian chile paste

1 tablespoon honey

1 teaspoon soy sauce or tamari

1 teaspoon fish sauce

1 teaspoon toasted sesame oil

1 lime

2 tablespoons coconut oil, divided

2 garlic cloves, thinly sliced

½ cup roasted unsalted peanuts, coarsely chopped

½ cup unsweetened coconut flakes

Pinch of crushed red pepper flakes

2 tablespoons neutral oil, such as grapeseed, sunflower, or safflower

1 pound asparagus, trimmed

½ cup fresh cilantro leaves and tender stems, torn, for serving

Searing tofu in large steaks is easy since it requires a lot less flipping. Here the tofu is browned, topped with a tangy chile sauce, then sprinkled with a crunchy peanut-and-coconut topping that makes a shaggy, golden, salty crust. The variety of textures is extremely satisfying, and the flavors are dynamic—a mix of sweet, spicy, toasty, and rich.

1. Arrange the tofu blocks on a clean kitchen towel or paper towels. Cover with another towel and place a heavy cutting board on top. Let the tofu drain for at least 10 minutes while you prep the other ingredients. Pat dry and season both sides of the tofu with salt and black pepper.

2. In a small bowl, add the sambal oelek, honey, soy sauce, fish sauce, sesame oil, and the finely grated zest of the lime. Cut the lime in half and squeeze one half into the sauce. Whisk well.

3. In a large skillet, heat 1 tablespoon of the coconut oil over medium-high heat. Add the garlic and cook until golden, 2 minutes. Stir in the peanuts, coconut flakes, a pinch of salt, and the red pepper flakes and cook until the coconut is lightly browned, 3 to 5 minutes. Remove from heat and squeeze the remaining lime half over everything. Transfer to a plate and wipe out the skillet.

4. Add the neutral oil to the skillet and heat over medium-high heat. When the oil shimmers, add the tofu in a single layer, in batches, if needed, and cook until golden, flipping the tofu when it releases easily from the pan (about 12 minutes total). Transfer the tofu to a paper towel–lined plate and tent foil on top to keep warm.

5. Add the remaining 1 tablespoon coconut oil and the asparagus to the pan. Reduce heat to medium and cook, covered, until tender, 2 to 3 minutes. Season with salt.

6. To serve, place the asparagus on a platter. Brush the sambal mixture thickly onto the tofu blocks and sprinkle generously with the peanut-coconut mixture to create a shaggy crust. Place the tofu on top of the asparagus and sprinkle with the cilantro. Serve any extra sambal sauce on the side.

SWAP IT OUT

Other quick-cooking green vegetables can stand in for the asparagus. Try sliced sugar snap peas or snow peas, thinly sliced brussels sprouts or cabbage, or sliced cucumber. Adjust the cooking time as needed depending on the vegetable.

Beets and Greens
Phyllo Pie

with Feta

SERVES 4

1 pound rainbow, red, or Swiss chard (1 to 2 bunches)

6 tablespoons (¾ stick) unsalted butter

2 garlic cloves, thinly sliced

½ teaspoon kosher salt, plus more as needed

8 ounces cooked, peeled beets, diced into ½-inch cubes (about 1 cup)

½ cup fresh dill, coarsely chopped

1 scallion, thinly sliced

Freshly ground black pepper

6 phyllo pastry sheets (from 1 package)

6 ounces Brie, hand torn into small pieces (including rind)

4 ounces feta, crumbled

Lemon wedges, for serving

Buying precooked beets makes this weeknight-friendly, but the crispy, buttery phyllo makes it feel like a weekend. If you're a fan of funky washed-rind cheeses, you can substitute taleggio or a ripe Camembert for the milder Brie. Goat cheese would also work well in place of the Brie, making the filling velvety rather than gooey, but just as delicious. And if you're starting with raw beets, see Swap It Out.

1. Place a sheet pan or pizza stone on the middle oven rack and heat the oven to 425°F.

2. Remove the chard stems and thinly slice them, discarding the ends. Tear the leaves into bite-size pieces and save for later.

3. In a large ovenproof skillet or sauté pan, melt the butter over medium heat. Pour most of the butter into a small bowl, leaving about 1 tablespoon or so in the pan. Add the garlic to the pan and sauté until the slices turn golden, 30 seconds to 1 minute. Add the chard stems and a big pinch of salt and continue to cook until the stems are tender and starting to brown, about 5 minutes. Add the chard leaves, tossing well, and let them cook until they wilt and any liquid in the pan dries out, 4 to 6 minutes.

4. Scrape the chard mixture into a large bowl. Add the beets, dill, scallion, ½ teaspoon salt, and a lot of pepper and toss to combine everything well.

5. Wipe out the skillet, let it cool for a few minutes (it can be warm, just not burning hot), then transfer it from the stove to a work surface or countertop. Brush the bottom and sides of the pan with some of the melted butter. Lay one sheet of phyllo in the skillet, gently pushing it down to fit without tearing, allowing the excess to hang over the edges of the pan. Gently brush the bottom and sides of the phyllo with more of the butter. Repeat with the remaining five phyllo sheets, buttering each layer as

SWAP IT OUT

Not a beet fan? Substitute 1 cup of any cooked, leftover vegetables you have around: sautéed mushrooms, peppers, or onions; roasted butternut squash, eggplant, broccoli, or cauliflower; steamed green beans or sugar snap peas. Or use some cooked sausage or ham in place of the beets to make this heartier.

If you're starting with raw beets, you'll need 12 ounces raw beets. Drizzle with olive oil, sprinkle with a little water, wrap in a double layer of foil, and place on a roasting pan. Roast at 350°F until tender, 1 to 2 hours, depending on the size of the beets. Peel while still warm.

you go and rotating them slightly so that the overhang falls at a different angle. Make sure to save a little of the butter for the top of the pie.

6. Spoon the chard-beet mixture in an even layer over the phyllo. Sprinkle the Brie and feta on top. Fold the overhanging phyllo over the filling (it won't cover it all the way, which is fine). Brush the phyllo on top with the remaining melted butter.

7. Place the skillet on the hot sheet pan or pizza stone and bake until the phyllo is golden brown and crisp, 20 to 25 minutes. Let the pie cool for 10 minutes before serving with lemon wedges for squeezing.

SKILLETS

Tartiflette

with Bitter Lettuces and Pear Salad

SERVES 6

FOR THE TARTIFLETTE

8 ounces smoked bacon, diced

2 medium yellow onions, diced (about 2½ cups)

2 garlic cloves, finely grated or minced

1 teaspoon finely chopped fresh thyme leaves

Pinch of freshly grated nutmeg

2 pounds Yukon Gold or other waxy potatoes, peeled and cut into 1-inch cubes (about 5½ cups)

¾ cup dry white wine (or use chicken or vegetable stock)

½ teaspoon kosher salt

½ teaspoon freshly ground black pepper

10 ounces soft cow's milk cheese with bloomy rind, such as Camembert or Brie

½ cup crème fraîche

This Alpine potato-and-bacon casserole is golden and gloriously gooey thanks to the slices of soft washed-rind cheese nestled on top before baking. Classic recipes have you boil the potatoes separately in one pot, brown the onion and bacon in a skillet, and then combine everything into a casserole dish for baking. This streamlined version accomplishes it all in one large skillet or sauté pan. I like to serve this with a leafy salad of peppery bitter greens to cut the richness.

1. Make the tartiflette: Heat the oven to 400°F.

2. Add the bacon to a cold large ovenproof skillet and place the pan over medium heat. Let the bacon cook, stirring occasionally, until the fat renders and the edges crisp slightly, 7 to 10 minutes.

3. Add the onions to the skillet and raise the heat to medium-high. Cook, stirring occasionally, until the onions are golden and soft, 7 to 10 minutes. Stir in the garlic, thyme, and nutmeg, and cook for another minute, until fragrant.

4. Add the potatoes, wine, salt, and pepper and toss until well combined. Cover the pan and cook, stirring occasionally, until the potatoes are just tender and the wine has mostly evaporated, 20 to 25 minutes. If the pan dries out while the potatoes are cooking, add a splash of water.

5. Slice the cheese ¼ inch thick (you can leave the rind on). Stir the crème fraîche into the potatoes, making sure they are evenly coated. Lay the cheese slices in an even layer on top of the potatoes. Bake, uncovered, until the cheese melts and the potatoes are very tender, 25 to 35 minutes. Serve hot or warm.

4 teaspoons sherry vinegar or apple cider vinegar, plus more to taste

¼ teaspoon kosher salt, plus more to taste

Large pinch of freshly ground black pepper

¼ cup extra-virgin olive oil

3 to 4 cups mixed bitter lettuces, such as endive, radicchio, frisée, or arugula

1 large ripe pear, cored and thinly sliced lengthwise

½ cup fresh parsley leaves

6. While the tartiflette is in the oven, **make the salad:** In a small bowl, whisk together the vinegar, salt, and pepper. Whisk in the oil. In a salad bowl, toss together the lettuces, pear, and parsley. Toss with enough of the dressing to coat everything. Taste and add more salt and vinegar, if needed. Serve alongside the tartiflette.

**CHEESY BAKED PASTA
WITH TOMATO, SAUSAGE,
AND RICOTTA, PAGE 106**

One-Pot Pastas
& Noodles

Cheesy Baked Pasta

with Tomato, Sausage, and Ricotta

SERVES 4

3 tablespoons extra-virgin olive oil

12 ounces hot or mild Italian sausage (pork, chicken, or turkey)

½ teaspoon fennel seeds

4 garlic cloves, thinly sliced

1 teaspoon dried oregano

Pinch of crushed red pepper flakes (optional), plus more for serving

1 (28-ounce) can whole peeled tomatoes

1 (14-ounce) can crushed or strained tomatoes

2 bay leaves

2 teaspoons kosher salt

12 ounces pasta (small shells, farfalle, or other small shape)

8 ounces fresh mozzarella, torn into bite-size pieces

6 ounces (about ¾ cup) whole-milk ricotta

⅓ cup grated Parmesan cheese

Freshly ground black pepper, for serving

¼ cup slivered fresh basil

Like a cross between baked ziti and a meaty lasagna, this golden-topped pasta is rich with brawny bits of sausage, creamy ricotta, and crushed tomatoes, all seasoned with plenty of garlic, oregano, and fennel seed. It's a certified crowd-pleaser that's easy to adapt.

1. Heat the oven to 425°F.

2. In a 12-inch ovenproof skillet or Dutch oven, heat the oil over medium-high heat. Remove the casings from the sausage and crumble the meat into skillet, using a spoon to break it up. Cook, stirring, until it's starting to brown, 5 to 7 minutes.

3. Using a mortar and pestle or the flat side of a chef's knife and a cutting board, lightly crush the fennel seeds. Stir them into the pan along with the garlic, oregano, and red pepper flakes, if using, and cook another 1 to 2 minutes.

4. Stir in the whole tomatoes, using a spoon to break them up. Add the crushed tomatoes, bay leaves, and salt and bring to a simmer. Cook for 10 minutes to thicken it slightly.

5. Stir in the pasta and 1 cup water and return the sauce to a simmer. Cook for 2 minutes, stirring to make sure the pasta doesn't stick to the pan. Remove from the heat, remove the bay leaves, and fold in a third of the mozzarella.

6. Top the pasta with the remaining mozzarella and dollops of ricotta. Sprinkle with the Parmesan. Bake until the pasta is tender when poked with a fork, and the cheese is bubbly and golden, 18 to 22 minutes. (If you'd like a browner topping, run the pan under the broiler for 1 to 2 minutes.) Let cool slightly before serving with black pepper and basil on top, and more red pepper flakes on the side.

VEGETARIAN UPGRADE

You can leave out the sausage entirely or substitute a plant-based sausage here.

VEG IT UP

You can add 8 ounces of sliced mushrooms along with the sausage in Step 2. Increase the cook time until the moisture evaporates from the pan, and everything is very browned.

Cheesy, Peppery Spaghetti

with Asparagus

SERVES 3 OR 4

1 tablespoon extra-virgin olive oil, plus more for drizzling

1 pound asparagus, trimmed and diagonally sliced ½ inch thick

1 garlic clove, finely grated or minced

1¾ teaspoons kosher salt, plus more as needed

1 pound spaghetti

1 cup grated pecorino Romano cheese, plus more for serving

½ cup grated Parmesan cheese

1½ tablespoons coarsely ground black pepper, plus more for serving

A nod to the classic Roman pasta dish cacio e pepe, this streamlined variation is especially creamy from being made in one pot, but still maintains its peppery bite. The asparagus, which is seared until lightly caramelized in spots, adds texture, color, and vegetable matter. Sugar snap peas or mushrooms will work equally well (see Swap It Out).

1. In a large skillet or sauté pan, heat the oil over medium-high heat. Add the asparagus and cook until golden brown, 2 to 3 minutes for thin asparagus, 4 to 5 minutes for thick asparagus. Stir in the garlic and ¼ teaspoon salt, and cook until fragrant, about 30 seconds. Using a slotted spoon, transfer the asparagus to a plate.

2. Return the skillet to medium-high heat and add 5 cups water and the remaining 1½ teaspoons salt and bring to a simmer. If the spaghetti won't lie flat in the skillet, break it in half. Add the spaghetti and cook, uncovered, stirring and tossing the pasta frequently, until it is cooked through but still al dente, 10 to 12 minutes. If the skillet dries out before the pasta is cooked through, add a little water.

3. Remove the pan from the heat and stir in the pecorino, Parmesan, and pepper, tossing well. Add the asparagus back into the pasta and toss to combine.

4. Serve immediately, sprinkled with additional grated pecorino and pepper, if you like, and drizzled with a little oil.

SWAP IT OUT

You can use 8 ounces sliced sugar snap peas or sliced mushrooms instead of the asparagus.

VEG IT UP

Adding 1 to 2 cups thawed frozen peas will increase the green factor and add sweetness. Alternatively, 1 cup halved cherry tomatoes seasoned with salt is a juicier addition. Add either one (or both!) in Step 3 along with the asparagus.

Bacon and Egg Spaghetti

with Greens and Herbs

SERVES 2 OR 3

2 large eggs

3 large egg yolks

½ cup grated Parmesan cheese

½ cup grated pecorino Romano cheese, plus more for serving

1 tablespoon freshly ground black pepper, plus more for serving

1½ teaspoons kosher salt, divided, plus more as needed

1 tablespoon extra-virgin olive oil

6 ounces bacon, diced

1 medium onion, diced

12 ounces spaghetti

8 ounces (about 8 cups) baby spinach, chopped

1 cup torn fresh basil leaves

1 cup torn fresh parsley leaves and tender stems

Inspired by the rich and porky goodness of spaghetti carbonara, this vegetable-focused pasta dish is loaded with spinach, basil, and parsley. It's just as creamy as the classic version but a lot more colorful and ever so slightly lighter.

1. In a medium bowl, whisk together the eggs, egg yolks, Parmesan, pecorino, pepper, and a pinch of salt. Set aside.

2. In a large sauté pan, heat the oil over medium heat. Add the bacon and cook, stirring occasionally, until the fat renders and the edges crisp, 8 to 10 minutes. Add the onion to the pan and raise the heat to medium-high. Cook, stirring occasionally, until the onion is golden brown and soft, 5 to 7 minutes.

3. If the spaghetti won't lie flat in the skillet, break it in half. Add it to the pan along with 4¾ cups of water and 1 teaspoon of the salt. Cook, uncovered, stirring and tossing the pasta frequently, until it is cooked through but still al dente, 12 to 14 minutes. If the skillet dries out before the pasta is cooked through, add a little water. The pan should stay moist; having a bit of extra pasta water in the pan will make for a creamier, silkier carbonara sauce.

4. Remove the pan from the heat and stir in the egg-cheese mixture, tossing well. Add the spinach, in batches as it begins to wilt, the basil, parsley, and remaining ½ teaspoon salt and energetically toss until everything is well incorporated. Cover the pan for 2 minutes to allow the spinach to fully cook. Uncover and toss again.

5. Serve immediately, sprinkled with pecorino and pepper.

VEG IT UP

Adding 1 cup or so of corn kernels (fresh, or frozen and thawed) along with the spinach gives this a sweetness that sets off the smoky bacon. Halved cherry tomatoes, seasoned with a pinch of salt, would lend a tart, juicy note.

VEGETARIAN UPGRADE

Substitute 8 ounces diced mushrooms for the bacon, letting the mushrooms get really brown before adding the onion. This takes it far away from carbonara territory, but it still tastes wonderful.

Spaghetti with Tuna

Capers and Cherry Tomatoes

SERVES 4

3 tablespoons extra-virgin olive oil, plus more for serving

4 garlic cloves, thinly sliced

3 scallions, thinly sliced (white and green parts separated)

3 oil-packed anchovy fillets, chopped (optional)

3 tablespoons capers, drained

2 cups quartered cherry tomatoes, divided

12 ounces spaghetti

¾ teaspoon kosher salt, plus more as needed

1 cup torn fresh herbs, such as parsley and dill, or celery leaves, plus more for serving

1 (5- or 6-ounce) can tuna, preferably oil-packed, drained and flaked

Lemon wedges, for serving

Crushed red pepper flakes, for serving (optional)

This dish has a rich and creamy tuna casserole vibe, but with a brighter, zippier flavor from the combination of capers, cherry tomatoes, and that jolt of lemon juice right at the end (and without any of the cheese). I like oil-packed tuna here for its richness, but water-packed will work just as well.

1. In a 12-inch sauté pan, heat the oil over medium heat. Add the garlic and scallion whites (save the greens for later) and cook until fragrant, about 2 minutes. Add the anchovies, if using, and the capers and cook until the anchovies dissolve and the garlic turns golden, 2 to 3 minutes longer. Add 1 cup of the cherry tomatoes and toss to evenly coat.

2. If the spaghetti won't lie flat in the pan, break it in half. Add it to the pan along with 4 cups of water and the salt. Raise the heat to medium-high and cook, stirring and tossing the pasta frequently, until it is cooked through but still al dente, 10 to 12 minutes. If the skillet dries out before the pasta is cooked through, add a little water. And if there's a bit of water left in the pan at the end, fear not, the pasta will absorb it in the next step. Just make sure to take the pan off the heat before the pasta gets too soft.

3. Remove the pan from the heat and stir in the remaining 1 cup tomatoes, the herbs, tuna, and scallion greens, and toss well. Season to taste with salt and the juice squeezed from a lemon wedge or two. Serve garnished with red pepper flakes, if you like, along with more herbs, lemon wedges, and a drizzle of oil.

VEG IT UP

Stir 4 to 5 cups (4 to 5 ounces) baby spinach or baby kale into the pasta along with the tuna in Step 3, letting the greens wilt. Or, add 1 cup shelled frozen edamame, sliced sugar snap peas, or green beans to the pan during the last five minutes of the pasta's cooking time in Step 2.

Cavatelli with Butternut Squash

Ricotta and Rosemary Brown Butter

SERVES 4

5 tablespoons unsalted butter

2 medium or 1 large shallot, thinly sliced (about ¾ cup)

1 pound butternut squash, peeled, trimmed, seeded, and cut into ¾-inch cubes (about 3 cups)

1 teaspoon finely chopped fresh rosemary leaves

2 teaspoons fine sea salt, plus more as needed

¼ teaspoon freshly ground black pepper

12 ounces cavatelli

½ cup whole-milk ricotta

⅓ cup chopped fresh mint, basil, dill, or parsley leaves and tender stems (or a mix), plus more for garnish

1 teaspoon grated lemon zest

Crushed red pepper flakes, for serving

Grated Parmesan cheese, for serving

The key to this gorgeously creamy pasta dish is to use a dense shape like cavatelli, which will cook in the same time it takes the squash to turn velvety soft and very sweet. Don't leave out the fresh herbs or red pepper flakes, which add essential freshness, verve, and color to the plate.

1. In a large skillet, melt the butter over medium heat. Cook, swirling occasionally, until the foam subsides, the milk solids turn golden brown, and it smells nutty and toasty, 3 to 4 minutes. (Watch carefully to see that it doesn't burn.)

2. Stir in the shallots and cook, stirring occasionally, until slightly softened, about 2 minutes. Add the squash, rosemary, a pinch of salt, and the black pepper and cook until the squash is golden at the edges and begins to soften, 5 to 7 minutes.

3. Add 3¼ cups water and salt to the pan and bring to a boil. Stir in cavatelli and reduce the heat to medium-low. Cover and cook until the pasta has absorbed all the water and is al dente, 18 to 25 minutes, depending on the brand. Stir occasionally to ensure the pasta does not stick to the bottom of the pan, and add more water, 1 tablespoon at a time, if the pan looks dry.

4. When the cavatelli is just cooked, remove the pan from the heat and stir in the ricotta, mint, and lemon zest. Taste and add more salt, if needed. Serve sprinkled with red pepper flakes, lots of Parmesan, and more chopped herbs.

SWAP IT OUT

For a more juicy variation, use 3 cups whole cherry tomatoes instead of the squash. And if you're looking for something heartier, substitute 1 tablespoon olive oil and 2 ounces diced pancetta for the butter, letting the cubes brown before adding the shallots.

VEG IT UP

Add 2 to 3 ounces (2 to 3 cups) of tender greens (baby spinach, chard, or arugula) to your pasta along with the ricotta, tossing until the greens wilt. Or, stir in ½ cup thawed frozen peas during the last 3 minutes of cooking, before adding the ricotta.

ONE-POT PASTAS & NOODLES

Lemony Orecchiette

with Chickpeas, Chile, and Arugula

SERVES 4

2 (15.5-ounce) cans chickpeas, drained and rinsed

½ cup plus 2 tablespoons extra-virgin olive oil, divided, plus more as needed

1½ teaspoons kosher salt, divided, plus more as needed

4 garlic cloves, smashed and peeled

1 medium onion or 2 shallots, diced

2 tablespoons finely chopped fresh rosemary

Pinch of crushed red pepper flakes, plus more as needed

1 pound orecchiette

5 ounces (5 cups) arugula

1 lemon

1¼ cups grated Parmesan cheese, plus more as needed

2 tablespoons unsalted butter

Freshly ground black pepper

VEG IT UP

This makes a nice pasta salad, served warm or at room temperature. Toss another 5 to 6 ounces (5 to 6 cups) arugula or other salad greens with a little olive oil, lemon juice, and salt, and spread it out on a platter. Top the greens with the orecchiette, then garnish with more olive oil, lemon juice, and pepper.

Mashing some of the chickpeas while leaving the rest whole makes this garlicky pasta very creamy, almost like mac and cheese. But instead of mild and milky, this is a whole lot zestier, with the lemon and arugula adding bracing notes, and the chile sparking things up. You can serve this as is for a filling, hearty meal, or plop the whole thing on some lightly dressed greens for a warm pasta salad that walks the line between light and rich (see Veg It Up).

1. Place half of the chickpeas, 2 tablespoons of the oil, and ½ teaspoon of the salt in a large bowl and use a potato masher or fork to mash. They should be crushed into a rough purée. Stir in the remaining chickpeas and set aside.

2. In a large skillet or Dutch oven, heat the remaining ½ cup oil over medium heat. Add the garlic and fry until golden brown, 4 to 5 minutes. Stir in the onion, rosemary, red pepper flakes, and a pinch of salt. Cook, stirring occasionally, until the onion is soft, 8 to 10 minutes.

3. Stir in the chickpea mixture and cook for 2 minutes. Raise the heat to medium-high and add 4½ cups water and the remaining 1 teaspoon salt. Bring to a simmer and add the orecchiette. Cook until the pasta is al dente, 15 to 17 minutes. Orecchiette can stick together if left unattended, which can result in uneven cooking, so stir frequently. If the pan dries out during cooking, add a little more water.

4. Remove the pan from the heat and stir in the arugula until wilted, 1 to 2 minutes. Grate the zest from the lemon directly into the pot. Cut the naked lemon into wedges and squeeze a wedge or two into the pot. Toss in the cheese and butter. Season to taste with black pepper, salt, red pepper flakes, and more lemon juice, if needed. Drizzle with oil and serve with more Parmesan and black pepper, if you like.

Orzo with Zucchini

Feta and Dill

SERVES 4

3 tablespoons unsalted butter

3 large or 4 to 5 small shallots, diced (about 1¼ cups)

1½ pounds zucchini, diced into ½-inch cubes (6 cups)

3 large garlic cloves, minced

1½ teaspoons kosher salt, divided, plus more to taste

3 cups vegetable stock

1½ cups orzo

1 lemon

1¼ cups crumbled feta (5 ounces), plus more for garnish

¾ cup frozen peas, thawed

1½ cups chopped fresh dill, parsley, or cilantro (or a combination), plus more for garnish

Extra-virgin olive oil, for serving

Crushed red pepper flakes, for serving

Creamy and tangy from the feta, bright from lemon zest, and full of tender bits of zucchini and sweet little green peas, this meatless main course is both cheesy and light, thanks to all the vegetables in the pan. If you're looking to add protein, shrimp would be an excellent choice (see Add It In).

1. Heat a large skillet over medium-high heat, then add the butter and let it melt. Stir in the shallots and zucchini, and cook, stirring occasionally, until browned and softened, about 8 minutes. Add the garlic and ½ teaspoon of the salt and cook until fragrant, 1 minute.

2. Stir in the stock and bring to a simmer, then add the orzo. Grate the lemon zest directly into the skillet, then add the remaining 1 teaspoon salt. Cover the pan and simmer over medium-low heat until the orzo is cooked through but al dente and most of the liquid is absorbed, 12 to 15 minutes, stirring once or twice. If the pan dries out toward the end, add a little more stock or water.

3. Stir in the feta, peas, and dill. Cover the pan and cook for another minute or two to warm the peas. Remove from the heat. Cut the zested lemon in half, and squeeze one of the halves into the pan. Taste and add more lemon juice and salt, if you like. Sprinkle with more feta, dill, oil, and red pepper flakes for serving.

SWAP IT OUT

Eggplant, peppers, or mushrooms can stand in for the zucchini. If you want to use fresh peas, add them in Step 2 during the last 5 minutes of cooking so they have a chance to cook through.

VEG IT UP

To add brightness and juiciness, stir in a cup of diced cherry tomatoes (seasoned with salt) just before serving. For a little extra sweetness, stir in ½ cup of corn kernels with the peas in Step 3.

ADD IT IN

Sauté a pound of fresh shrimp in the butter in Step 1 until they turn pink (3 to 6 minutes), then transfer them to a plate while you cook the vegetables and orzo. Return them to the pan along with the peas in Step 3.

ONE-POT PASTAS & NOODLES

Creamy Goat Cheese Pasta

with Burst Cherry Tomatoes and Olives

SERVES 4

Kosher salt

1 pound short pasta (such as orecchiette, farfalle, fusilli, or rigatoni)

6 tablespoons extra-virgin olive oil, divided, plus more for serving

5 garlic cloves, thinly sliced

4 cups halved cherry tomatoes, divided

½ cup chopped pitted green olives (such as Castelvetrano)

1 teaspoon fresh thyme leaves

½ teaspoon freshly ground black pepper

Pinch of crushed red pepper flakes, plus more for serving

6 ounces goat cheese, broken up into small pieces

½ cup heavy cream

¼ cup grated Parmesan cheese, plus more for serving

1 cup torn fresh basil leaves

SWAP IT OUT

For a milder dish, try substituting fresh ricotta or a combination of cream cheese and cheddar, for the goat cheese, and adding some grated lemon zest at the end if you'd like to brighten it up.

This one-pot pasta uses a slightly different technique than the others in this chapter. Instead of starting the sauce in the skillet, then adding the dried pasta to cook in the sauce, here I cook the pasta first, drain it, then quickly mix together a creamy goat cheese sauce right in the pasta pot. It's a lot like making one-pot mac and cheese, except with the more sophisticated flavors of goat cheese, olives, and garlicky tomatoes.

1. Bring a large pot of salted water to a boil. Add the pasta and cook until 1 minute shy of al dente (check the package directions for timing). Drain the pasta, reserving ½ cup pasta cooking water.

2. Place the pot over medium-high heat and add 4 tablespoons of the oil. Add the garlic and cook until golden, about 2 minutes. Stir in about half the tomatoes, the olives, thyme, ½ teaspoon salt, black pepper, and red pepper flakes. Cook until the tomatoes just begin to soften, 3 to 5 minutes.

3. Reduce the heat to low and stir in the goat cheese and cream, letting it melt into a sauce. Remove from the heat and stir in the drained pasta, the remaining tomatoes, Parmesan, and remaining 2 tablespoons oil and toss until evenly coated. If the mixture looks dry, add a little pasta cooking water, a tablespoon at a time. Taste a piece of pasta to make sure it's cooked through (if not, put the pot back on the heat for another minute or so, stirring). Stir in the basil.

4. To serve, top the pasta with more Parmesan, red pepper flakes, and oil.

Pasta with Garlicky Broccoli Rabe

Lemon Zest and Mozzarella

SERVES 4

1 bunch (about 1 pound) broccoli rabe

3 tablespoons extra-virgin olive oil, plus more for serving

4 garlic cloves, thinly sliced

4 to 8 oil-packed anchovy fillets, chopped

Pinch of crushed red pepper flakes, plus more for serving

1 pound short pasta, such as gemelli, orecchiette, or fusilli

1 teaspoon kosher salt, plus more to taste

½ cup torn fresh basil leaves (or use parsley or mint)

1 lemon

4 ounces fresh mozzarella, torn into 1-inch pieces (about 1 cup)

Flaky sea salt, for serving

VEG IT UP

Add 1 or 2 cups of halved cherry tomatoes seasoned with a little salt, or ½ cup sliced roasted red peppers, at the very end, along with the lemon juice (after you've added the mozzarella). This adds great color to the mix. Or, to contribute a little sweetness, stir in ½ cup fresh or frozen corn kernels or peas along with the broccoli rabe.

Luscious and gooey from the mozzarella, pungent from the garlic, and filled with silky, olive oil-imbued greens, this pasta is a total crowd-pleaser, especially if you forget to mention the anchovies in the sauce (no one will know they're there if you don't tell them). If you want to elevate this to even creamier heights, substitute burrata, which is cheese layered with cream, for the mozzarella.

1. Trim away the thick, tough stems from the broccoli rabe and discard them. Slice the tender stems and leaves into ½-inch lengths. Leave the florets whole. You should have 7 to 8 cups.

2. In a large skillet, heat the oil over medium heat. Add the garlic, anchovies, and red pepper flakes and cook until the garlic turns lightly golden at the edges, 1 to 2 minutes. Stir in the broccoli rabe.

3. Add the pasta, 4½ cups water, and the kosher salt to the pan. Let the water come to a boil, then cover the pan. Cook, stirring and tossing the pasta once or twice, until it is cooked through but still al dente, 10 to 12 minutes. If the skillet dries out before the pasta is cooked through, add a little water. And if there's a bit of water left in the pan at the end, fear not, the pasta will absorb it in the next step. Just make sure to take the pan off the heat before the pasta gets too soft.

4. Remove the pan from the heat and stir in the basil. Grate 1 teaspoon lemon zest directly into the pan, then add the mozzarella and toss well. Season to taste with kosher salt. Cut the zested lemon in half and squeeze in lemon juice to taste. Serve garnished with more red pepper flakes, if you like, along with flaky sea salt and a drizzle of oil.

VEGAN UPGRADE

Substitute ¼ cup finely chopped kalamata olives for the anchovies and then skip the cheese at the end (it's nice here but not at all necessary).

Skillet Shrimp Scampi

with Orzo and Tomatoes

SERVES 2 OR 3

2 tablespoons unsalted butter

2 tablespoons extra-virgin olive oil, plus more for serving

4 garlic cloves, finely grated or minced

½ cup dry white wine or stock

1¾ teaspoons kosher salt, divided

½ teaspoon freshly ground black pepper

⅛ teaspoon crushed red pepper flakes, plus more for serving

1 pound large or extra-large shrimp, peeled and deveined

1 cup orzo

1 cup halved cherry tomatoes

½ cup chopped fresh parsley leaves and tender stems

1 lemon, halved

Flaky sea salt, for serving

VEG IT UP

Add up to 1 cup of (thawed) frozen corn kernels or peas along with the tomatoes in Step 4. If you want to add greens, chopped spinach, baby chard, or mustard greens would work well. Fold 3 to 4 ounces (3 to 4 cups) into the pan during the last few minutes of cooking in Step 3.

If you're a fan of the buttery, garlicky, wine-soaked flavors of shrimp scampi, you'll love this one-pot version, in which orzo soaks up all that glorious sauce. The orzo gets very creamy as it cooks, almost like risotto but with the rich, familiar flavor of pasta. To add color and more vegetables to the pan, throw in some peas, greens, or corn kernels right at the end (see Veg It Up).

1. In a large sauté pan or skillet, melt the butter with the oil over medium-high heat. Add the garlic and sauté until fragrant, about 1 minute. Add the wine, ½ teaspoon of the kosher salt, the black pepper, and red pepper flakes, and bring to a simmer. Let the wine reduce by half, about 2 minutes.

2. Add the shrimp and sauté until they just turn pink, 2 to 4 minutes, depending upon their size. Using a slotted spoon, transfer the shrimp to a plate and tent with foil to keep it warm.

3. Add 2 cups of water to the skillet and bring to a simmer. Stir in the orzo and 1 teaspoon of the kosher salt. Cover the pan and let the orzo simmer over medium-low heat until it is just tender and most of the liquid is absorbed, 12 to 15 minutes, stirring once or twice. If the pan dries out toward the end, add a little more water.

4. Return the shrimp to the pan, along with the tomatoes and the remaining ¼ teaspoon kosher salt and cook for 2 minutes. Stir in the parsley and then squeeze in the juice from half the lemon, gently tossing to combine. Cut the remaining lemon half into wedges for serving.

5. Serve the orzo sprinkled with flaky sea salt and more red pepper flakes, if you like, and drizzled with a little oil, with the lemon wedges on the side.

Spiced Pearl Couscous

with Jammy Eggplant and Tomatoes

SERVES 4

7 tablespoons extra-virgin olive oil, divided, plus more for serving

2 medium yellow onions, thinly sliced (about 4 cups)

1¼ pounds Italian eggplant, cut into 1-inch cubes

2 teaspoons kosher salt

½ teaspoon freshly ground black pepper

4 garlic cloves, finely grated or minced

2 teaspoons ground cinnamon

1 teaspoon ground cumin

½ teaspoon sweet paprika

½ teaspoon smoked paprika

2 cups pearl couscous

1 (14.5-ounce) can diced tomatoes

1 cup fresh basil leaves, coarsely chopped, plus more for garnish

1 cup fresh mint leaves, coarsely chopped, plus more for garnish

Labneh or Greek yogurt, for serving

Flaky sea salt, for serving

SWAP IT OUT

Feta is a nice, saltier substitute for the labneh.

Pearl couscous—which we've been calling "pasta bubbles" ever since our daughter, Dahlia, was a toddler—is an ideal one-pot meal. Here, inspired by a recipe from Adeena Sussman's wonderful Israeli cookbook, *Sababa*, I've added a bevy of spices, plus sautéed eggplant and cherry tomatoes that cook down into a soft, savory jam. Don't stint on the herbs and labneh (or yogurt); they're essential, lending verve and creaminess right at the end.

1. Heat a 12-inch skillet over medium-high heat. Add 3 tablespoons of the oil and let it heat for a few seconds, until it thins out to coat the pan, then add the onions. Cook, stirring occasionally, until softened and golden, about 6 minutes.

2. Add the eggplant, 1 teaspoon of the kosher salt, the pepper, and the remaining 4 tablespoons oil to the pan. Cook, stirring once or twice, until the eggplant is browned, about 10 minutes. Add the garlic, cinnamon, cumin, and sweet and smoked paprikas and stir until fragrant, about 1 minute.

3. Stir in the couscous, tomatoes, remaining 1 teaspoon salt, and 2¾ cups water, cover, reduce the heat to low, and simmer until the couscous has absorbed all the liquid and is tender, 10 to 14 minutes. Stir occasionally while cooking, scraping up any bits that stick to the bottom of the pan. Add more water, 1 tablespoon at a time, if the pan seems dry. Turn off the heat and let the couscous rest, covered, for 2 minutes. Uncover and add the basil and mint, tossing until well combined.

4. Serve immediately, dolloped with labneh, sprinkled with flaky salt and more herbs, and drizzled with oil.

VEG IT UP

Stir in 4 to 5 cups (4 to 5 ounces) baby spinach right at the end of Step 3, before letting the mixture rest. For additional creaminess, this is wonderful served with avocado slices on the side.

ADD IT IN

If you want to add protein, sauté ½ pound of ground meat—lamb, beef, turkey—with the onions once they're translucent in Step 1. Let it get brown before adding the eggplant in Step 2.

Gingery Coconut Noodles

with Shrimp and Greens

SERVES 4

6 ounces wide rice noodles (aka rice linguine or rice sticks)

2 tablespoons coconut oil or neutral oil, such as grapeseed, sunflower, or safflower

6 scallions, thinly sliced (white and green parts separated)

2 jalapeños, seeded if you like: 1 minced, 1 thinly sliced

½ teaspoon kosher salt, divided, plus more as needed

4 garlic cloves, finely grated or minced, divided

2 tablespoons finely grated or minced fresh ginger, divided

1 pound large shrimp, peeled and deveined

1 (13.5-ounce) can unsweetened full-fat coconut milk

2 tablespoons fish sauce, plus more to taste

1 lime

5 ounces (about 5 cups) baby spinach

1 cup chopped fresh cilantro or basil leaves (or a combination), plus more for garnish

Simmering rice noodles in coconut milk makes them slightly sweet and very creamy, and a perfect foil for the loads of ginger, lime, and herbs that go into the sauce of this lively dish. Here the piquant noodles are topped with soft, gently cooked shrimp to add protein and color. But salmon fillets will work just as well, if you happen to have those on hand instead (see Swap It Out).

1. Put the rice noodles in a large bowl and add enough hot tap water to cover. Set aside while prepping the other ingredients.

2. In a large skillet, heat the oil over medium heat. Stir in the scallion whites and minced jalapeño (save the scallion greens and jalapeño slices for garnish). Add a large pinch of salt and cook until everything is starting to brown, about 5 minutes.

3. Stir half the garlic and half the ginger into the pan (save the remaining garlic and ginger for the coconut milk). Cook until fragrant, about 1 minute.

4. Add the shrimp to the pan along with ¼ teaspoon of the salt and sauté until the shrimp turns pink and is just cooked through, 3 to 5 minutes. Using a slotted spoon, transfer the shrimp to a plate and tent with foil to keep it warm (leave any solids not clinging to the shrimp in the pan).

5. Stir the coconut milk and fish sauce into the pan and add the remaining garlic and ginger. Grate the zest from the lime into the pan. (Cut the zested lime into wedges to save for serving.) Bring the coconut milk to a gentle simmer and cook for 2 minutes to blend the flavors.

6. Drain the noodles and rinse with cold water. Add the noodles to the skillet and toss well. Stir in the spinach and remaining ¼ teaspoon salt and cook, covered, until the noodles are al dente and the spinach is wilted, 7 to 9 minutes, stirring occasionally. (If the pan starts to dry out before the noodles cook through, add a few splashes of water to the pan.) Remove the pan from the heat and add the shrimp, cilantro, and the reserved scallion greens, tossing everything until well combined. Taste and add more salt, fish sauce, and a squeeze of lime.

7. Serve garnished with more herbs, the jalapeño slices, and lime wedges for squeezing.

SWAP IT OUT

You can substitute 1 pound salmon fillets for the shrimp. Season them with ½ teaspoon salt and a pinch of black pepper and sauté them in Step 4 for 7 to 10 minutes, depending on thickness. Transfer the salmon to a plate and continue with the recipe, serving the salmon on top of the noodles.

VEG IT UP

You can double the spinach, sprinkling on a little more fish sauce to add depth.

Crispy Chile-Glazed Tofu

with Soba Noodles

SERVES 4

1 (14-ounce) package firm tofu, drained

1 small bunch scallions, trimmed

3 tablespoons neutral oil, such as grapeseed, sunflower, or safflower, divided

2 tablespoons toasted sesame oil, divided

3 garlic cloves, thinly sliced

2 teaspoons finely grated or minced fresh ginger

¼ cup soy sauce or tamari

3 tablespoons dark brown sugar

1 teaspoon freshly ground black pepper

¼ teaspoon crushed red pepper flakes

1 (8-ounce) package all-buckwheat soba noodles

1 tablespoon fresh lime juice, plus lime wedges for serving

1½ cups thinly sliced seedless cucumber (Persian or hothouse)

2 to 4 radishes, thinly sliced

Handful of fresh cilantro leaves, for serving

The most time-consuming part about making these sweet and spicy noodles is pan-frying the tofu. But those crunchy, salty tofu cubes are my favorite part of the dish, and I think well worth the effort. If you're looking for a shortcut, substitute baked or seasoned tofu for the plain firm kind (see Swap It Out). You'll slash about 15 minutes off the prep time—and still be left with a gorgeous panful of savory buckwheat noodles and colorful veggies seasoned with tangy lime, ginger, and sesame.

1. Pat the tofu dry with a clean kitchen towel or paper towels. Cover with another kitchen towel and place a heavy cutting board on top. Let the tofu drain for about 10 minutes while you prep the remaining ingredients.

2. Cut the scallions into 2-inch lengths, then slice the pieces lengthwise into matchsticks, separating the white and green parts.

3. Cut the tofu into 1-inch cubes. Heat a large skillet over medium-high heat and add 2 tablespoons of the neutral oil and 1 tablespoon of the sesame oil. When the oil shimmers, add the tofu in a single layer, in batches, if needed, and cook until golden on all sides, flipping the tofu when it releases easily from the pan (about 12 minutes total). Transfer the tofu to a paper towel–lined plate and tent foil on top to keep it warm.

4. Add the remaining 1 tablespoon neutral oil and 1 tablespoon sesame oil, the garlic, ginger, and scallion whites and cook until fragrant, stirring constantly, about 1 minute. Add the soy sauce, sugar, black pepper, red pepper flakes, and 2 cups water and bring to a boil. Stir in the soba noodles, reduce the heat to medium-low, and cook at a simmer, covered, until the noodles are al dente, stirring occasionally, 6 to 8 minutes. Adjust the heat as needed and add more water if the pan looks dry.

5. Add the scallion greens and tofu to the noodles and gently toss until everything is well mixed and covered with sauce. Remove from the heat and add the lime juice, tossing to combine. Garnish with cucumber and radish slices, and cilantro on top. Serve warm or at room temperature, with lime wedges on the side for squeezing.

SWAP IT OUT

Instead of frying the firm tofu, substitute a 12- to 16-ounce package of baked or seasoned tofu, cut into cubes. Toss it in the pan with the noodles in Step 4.

VEG IT UP

Serve this on a bed of sliced cabbage or hardy salad greens (like baby kale) that has been dressed with a squeeze of lime juice, a pinch of salt, and a drizzle of toasted sesame oil. Or season 1 or 2 cups of halved cherry tomatoes with soy sauce and sesame oil, then toss them into the pan along with the tofu in Step 5.

Dutch
Ovens

Tender Chicken in a Pot

with Pearl Couscous, Lemon, and Mint

___

SERVES 4

1 whole chicken (about
3½ pounds), patted dry

2 teaspoons kosher salt,
divided, plus more as needed

½ teaspoon freshly ground
black pepper

2 tablespoons extra-virgin
olive oil, divided, plus more for
serving

2 leeks, white and light green
parts, halved lengthwise and
thinly sliced into half moons

3 medium carrots, sliced into
½-inch coins

2 lemons

4 garlic cloves, minced or
finely grated

3 fresh thyme branches

¼ teaspoon crushed red
pepper flakes, plus more for
serving

1¾ cups pearl couscous

1 cup peas, fresh or frozen
(no need to thaw)

¾ cup fresh torn mint leaves
and tender stems (or use
cilantro or parsley), plus more
for serving

1 cup crumbled ricotta salata
or feta or grated Parmesan
cheese, for serving (optional)

Simmering a whole chicken in a pot surrounded by
vegetables and herbs makes the meat falling-off-the-bones
tender and deeply flavorful. In this dish, I add pearl couscous
to the broth, which is seasoned with loads of lemon zest
and juice, some red pepper flakes, plus mint for freshness.
I also like to fold crumbled or grated cheese in at the end
for richness and tang. But you can skip it for a slightly
lighter dish.

1. Heat the oven to 350°F. Season the chicken inside and out
with 1½ teaspoons of the salt and the black pepper. Let sit at
room temperature while preparing the other ingredients.

2. Heat a 5- or 6-quart Dutch oven over medium-high heat and
add 1 tablespoon of the oil. When the oil thins out and coats
the bottom of the pot, add the chicken, breast side down, and
sear until browned, 4 to 6 minutes. Transfer the chicken, breast
side up, to a plate (you don't need to sear any other parts of
the bird).

3. Add the remaining 1 tablespoon oil to the pot and stir in
the leeks, carrots, and a large pinch of salt. Sauté until the
vegetables are starting to brown, about 5 minutes.

4. Grate the zest from the lemons into the pot and add the
garlic, thyme, and red pepper flakes, and cook until fragrant,
1 to 2 minutes. Push the vegetables to the sides of the pot to
make room for the chicken.

5. Nestle the chicken, breast side up, amid the vegetables,
making sure the chicken is surrounded by them but not on top
of them (the chicken should touch the bottom of the pot). Pour
5 cups of water into the pot around the chicken. Continue to
add more water until the liquid comes up about two-thirds of
the leg of the chicken, keeping the browned breast above water.

6. Bring the liquid in the pot to a boil. Remove from the heat,
cover, and transfer to the oven. Bake for 1 hour.

(recipe continues)

VEG IT UP

Add 4 to 5 ounces (4 to 5 cups) chopped baby greens, like spinach, kale, or chard, to the couscous along with the shredded chicken and mint in Step 8, stirring until the greens wilt.

7. Carefully, take the pot out of the oven. Cut 1 naked lemon in half and squeeze the lemon juice into the pot. Add the couscous, peas, and remaining ½ teaspoon salt around the edges of the chicken and stir. Cover and continue to cook in the oven until the couscous has absorbed most of the liquid and is tender, 15 to 20 minutes. Remove from the oven and let rest for 10 minutes.

8. Uncover the pot and transfer the chicken to a plate or cutting board. Using two forks, shred the chicken into chunks and stir it back into the Dutch oven along with the mint. Taste and add more lemon juice from the remaining lemon and more salt, if needed.

9. To serve, spoon the chicken and couscous into bowls and generously sprinkle with the cheese, if you like, plus more mint, red pepper flakes, and oil.

Cumin-y Chicken and Rice

with Peppers and Peas

SERVES 4

3 tablespoons extra-virgin olive oil, divided, plus more as needed

2 fat garlic cloves, grated or minced

2 teaspoons ground cumin

2¼ teaspoons kosher salt, divided, plus more to taste

1½ pounds boneless, skinless chicken (either breasts or thighs)

1 medium red onion, diced

2 teaspoons tomato paste

½ teaspoon dried oregano

1½ cups long-grain white rice, rinsed

2½ cups chicken stock, homemade (page 247) or store-bought

2 bay leaves

½ cup frozen peas, thawed

½ cup roasted red peppers, drained and chopped

1 cup fresh cilantro leaves and tender stems, coarsely chopped

3 scallions, thinly sliced

Lime wedges, for serving

A nod to Cuban chicken and rice, this heady, spicy dish calls for boneless thighs or breasts instead of the usual bone-in pieces, making it weeknight-fast yet thoroughly savory. When serving this, don't forget to dig down and scoop up some of the crunchy browned rice sticking to the bottom of the pan. It's my favorite part.

1. In a large bowl, combine 1 tablespoon of the oil, the garlic, cumin, and 1½ teaspoons of the salt. Add the chicken, rubbing the paste all over it, and let it sit for 10 to 30 minutes at room temperature (use this time to gather the other ingredients).

2. In a 5- or 6-quart Dutch oven, heat the remaining 2 tablespoons oil over medium heat. Arrange the chicken in a single layer and cook until lightly browned, about 2 minutes on each side. Transfer the pieces to a plate as they brown.

3. Stir in the onion and remaining ¾ teaspoon salt. Cook until lightly browned, stirring occasionally, about 5 minutes, scraping up any browned bits on the bottom of the pot. (Reduce the heat if the oil starts to burn.) Stir in the tomato paste and oregano and cook another 30 seconds.

4. Add more oil if the pot looks dry, then stir in the rice and toss to coat the rice with oil. Add the stock and bay leaves, cover the pot, and bring the liquid to a boil. Reduce the heat to low and simmer for 5 minutes.

5. Return the chicken and any juices accumulated on the plate to the pot. Cover again and simmer on low until the rice and chicken are cooked through, 17 to 20 minutes.

6. Transfer the chicken to a cutting board and tent with foil to keep it warm. Taste the rice and add a little more salt, if needed. Remove the bay leaves, then stir the peas and peppers into the rice, fluffing it as you stir. Cover and let sit for 5 minutes.

7. Slice the chicken and serve it with the rice (scraping it up to get at the yummy browned bits sticking to the bottom of the pan), topped with cilantro and scallions and a generous squeeze of lime juice.

(see following page for tips)

ADD IT IN

Although it's not at all necessary, diced spicy pepperoni or chorizo (the cured variety that's like salami) makes an excellently porky addition. Add about 2 ounces to the pot with the onion in Step 3.

VEG IT UP

Stir 4 to 5 ounces (4 to 5 cups) baby spinach, or 1 to 2 cups halved cherry tomatoes, seasoned with a little salt, into the rice along with the peas and peppers.

Crispy Chicken Thighs

with Puttanesca Green Beans

SERVES 2 TO 4

4 boneless, skinless chicken thighs (about 1½ pounds)

Kosher salt and freshly ground black pepper

1 teaspoon **dried oregano**

3 tablespoons **extra-virgin olive oil**, divided, plus more for drizzling

1 large or 2 small **shallots**, thinly sliced

2 **garlic cloves**, thinly sliced

1 tablespoon **tomato paste**

12 ounces **green beans**, trimmed

3 tablespoons **chicken stock**, homemade (page 247) or store-bought, or **water**

¼ cup good **tangy olives**, pitted and coarsely chopped (use any kind you like, but Castelvetrano or kalamata are terrific)

1 tablespoon **brine-packed capers**, drained

Handful of torn **fresh parsley or cilantro leaves**, for serving

Crushed red pepper flakes, for serving (optional)

Briny olives, sweet browned shallots, and a dollop of tomato paste turn a pot full of green beans into something rich, savory, and impossible to stop eating. Here, the beans are roasted underneath boneless, skinless chicken thighs, which crisp up in the oven, turning golden on top and soft underneath.

1. Heat the oven to 425°F. Season the chicken all over with salt, black pepper, and the oregano.

2. Heat a 5- or 6-quart Dutch oven over medium-high heat, then add 1 tablespoon of the oil. When the oil thins out and coats the bottom of the pot, add the chicken and sear until browned on both sides, 5 to 7 minutes per side. Transfer the chicken to a plate.

3. Reduce the heat to medium and add the remaining 2 tablespoons oil to the pot. Add the shallot and a pinch of salt and sauté until the shallot is tender and golden brown, 2 minutes. Add the garlic and sauté until it browns at the edges, 1 to 2 minutes longer.

4. Add the tomato paste and sauté until it darkens and caramelizes around the shallot and garlic pieces, 30 seconds to 1 minute. Stir in the green beans and cook, stirring and scraping up all the dark bits at the bottom of the pan, until the beans get more vibrant in color and start to lighten in spots, 2 to 3 minutes. Stir in the stock, olives, and capers, again stirring and scraping the bottom of the pot. Put the chicken on top of the beans, pouring in any juices from the plate, and drizzle with a little more oil. Roast, uncovered, until the chicken is cooked through and the beans are tender, 20 to 25 minutes.

5. Transfer the chicken onto plates. Give the green beans a good toss in all the yummy pan juices at the bottom of the Dutch oven and pile them on top of the chicken. Sprinkle with the herbs and red pepper flakes, if you like.

SWAP IT OUT

A bunch of broccolini or two sliced fennel bulbs can stand in for the green beans.

Turkey and Bean Tamale Pie

SERVES 4 TO 6

A tamale pie has little to do with an actual Latin American tamale. But the layered chili and corn bread casserole is an American classic, the kind of retro comfort food you wax nostalgic for whether it was part of your childhood or not. Here is my take on the dish, streamlined into the coziest of one-pot meals. I like this dolloped with a little sour cream or yogurt, but it's purely optional.

FOR THE CHILI

3 tablespoons extra-virgin olive oil

1 pound ground turkey

1 large onion, finely chopped

Kosher salt and freshly ground black pepper

2 garlic cloves, minced

1 jalapeño, seeded if you like, chopped

2 tablespoons chili powder

1¼ teaspoons ground cumin

1 (15-ounce) can pinto beans (or use any kind of bean you like), drained and rinsed

1 (14.5-ounce) can whole plum or diced tomatoes

1 cup chopped fresh cilantro leaves and tender stems

SWAP IT OUT

Any kind of ground meat—beef, pork, lamb, or chicken—can stand in for the turkey. Sausage meat squeezed out of its casings works well here, too.

VEGETARIAN UPGRADE

Substitute another can of drained, rinsed beans for the ground turkey. Or substitute vegan meat.

VEG IT UP

Stir 1 cup of corn kernels into the corn bread mixture along with the scallions in Step 4. Or, you can add the corn to the chili mixture, which is a traditional way to go. Add it with the beans in Step 3. For something green, stir 4 to 5 cups (4 to 5 ounces) baby spinach or kale into the chili mixture along with the cilantro in Step 3.

(recipe continues)

¾ cup fine cornmeal

2 tablespoons all-purpose flour

1½ teaspoons baking powder

½ teaspoon kosher salt

1 large egg

⅓ cup milk

4 tablespoons melted unsalted butter or neutral oil, such as grapeseed, sunflower, or safflower

2 teaspoons honey

2 scallions, thinly sliced (optional), plus more for serving

1 cup grated cheddar cheese (optional)

Sour cream or yogurt, for serving

1. Heat the oven to 425°F.

2. Make the chili: In a 5- or 6-quart Dutch oven, heat the oil over medium-high heat. Add the turkey, onion, and a generous pinch each of salt and pepper and sauté until the meat is golden brown and the onion translucent, about 10 minutes.

3. Add the garlic and jalapeño to the pot and cook until fragrant, 2 to 3 minutes. Stir in the chili powder and cumin and let the spices cook until they darken, about 30 seconds. Add the beans and tomatoes, using a pair of kitchen shears to cut them up if using whole tomatoes (you can do this while they are still in the can, or after you've added them to the pot). Season with more salt and pepper and let the mixture simmer for 8 to 12 minutes, until thick and chili-like. Stir in the cilantro, then taste and add more salt and pepper, if needed.

4. While the chili is cooking, **prepare the corn bread:** In a medium bowl, whisk together the cornmeal, flour, baking powder, and salt. In a small bowl, whisk together the egg, milk, butter, and honey. Whisk the egg mixture into the cornmeal mixture until combined, then whisk in the scallions, if using.

5. Spread the corn bread topping over the chili, then top with the cheese, if using. The topping will disappear into the meat mixture but will rise during baking and form a layer of corn bread. Bake, uncovered, until the corn bread is brown, 20 to 25 minutes. Serve hot or warm, dolloped with sour cream or yogurt and sprinkled with scallions.

Wine-Braised Mushrooms and Gnocchi

SERVE 4 TO 6

5 tablespoons unsalted butter or extra-virgin olive oil, divided, plus more as needed

1¼ pounds mixed mushrooms, such as portobello, cremini, white button, shiitake, or oyster, cut into 1-inch chunks (about 6 cups)

Kosher salt and freshly ground black pepper

2 leeks, white and light green parts, halved lengthwise and thinly sliced into half moons

3 garlic cloves: 2 minced, 1 grated

1 tablespoon tomato paste

½ teaspoon smoked paprika, plus more for serving

1 cup dry red wine

2 cups vegetable stock

1 tablespoon tamari or soy sauce, plus more to taste

4 large fresh thyme branches or 2 fresh rosemary sprigs (or use both)

1 bay leaf

12 ounces gnocchi (fresh, frozen, or shelf-stable all work)

Sour cream or lemon wedges, for serving

Chopped fresh dill or parsley, for serving

Adding tender pillows of potato gnocchi to a pot of wine-braised mushrooms turns a meatless stew into a complex and comforting one-pot meal. As they cook, the gnocchi release starch into the broth, thickening it into a silky sauce that's rich with the caramelized notes of seared mushrooms and onions, along with a smoky tang from the paprika. Try to use a variety of different mushrooms here, so each can add its own distinct flavor and texture to the mix.

1. Add 2 tablespoons of the butter to a 5- or 6-quart Dutch oven and set it over medium heat. When the butter is melted and hot, stir in half the mushrooms. (If they don't all fit in the pot in one layer, you might have to do this in three batches, rather than two, so the mushrooms brown.) Without moving them around too much, cook the mushrooms until they are brown on one side, about 4 minutes. Stir and let them brown on the other side, 3 to 4 minutes more. Use a slotted spoon to transfer the mushrooms to a large bowl or plate and sprinkle with salt and pepper. Repeat with another 2 tablespoons of the butter and the remaining mushrooms, seasoning them as you go.

2. Reduce the heat to medium-low. Add the remaining 1 tablespoon butter to the pan. Add the leeks and sauté until they turn lightly golden and start to soften, 8 minutes. Add the minced garlic and a big pinch of salt and sauté for 1 minute longer. Stir in the tomato paste and smoked paprika and cook for 1 minute. Add the wine, stock, tamari, thyme, and bay leaf, scraping up the brown bits on the bottom of the pot.

3. Add the cooked mushrooms back to the pot and bring to a simmer. Partially cover the pot and continue simmering over low heat for 15 minutes. Stir in the gnocchi and simmer, partially covered, until the mushrooms are tender, the gnocchi are cooked, and the sauce is thick, about 30 minutes. Stir in the grated garlic. Taste and add more salt and tamari, if needed, then remove the bay leaf and thyme branches.

4. To serve, dollop each bowl of stew with sour cream or add a squeeze of lemon (this dish needs the acidity). Sprinkle the top with herbs and more smoked paprika.

Roasted Tuna

with Brown Butter Corn, Tomatoes, and Chile

SERVES 4

1½ pounds **tuna**, cut into steaks about 1 inch thick

½ teaspoon **kosher salt**, plus more as needed

Freshly ground **black pepper**

2 **garlic cloves**, minced or finely grated

1 teaspoon **ancho chile powder** (or substitute another chile powder)

4 tablespoons (½ stick) **unsalted butter**

5 **scallions**, thinly sliced (white and green parts separated)

2 **jalapeños**, seeded and diced

2 cups **corn kernels**, fresh (from about 2 ears) or frozen and thawed

1 pint **cherry tomatoes**, halved

1 tablespoon **extra-virgin olive oil**

Lime wedges, for serving

Flaky sea salt, for serving

A little like a confit, the tuna in this recipe gets gently cooked surrounded by brown butter–imbued corn spiked with chiles. Cherry tomatoes add a sweet juiciness to the pan while a squeeze of lime right at the end brightens everything up. It's a dish that seems to scream summer but tastes nearly as good in winter using frozen corn.

1. Heat the oven to 325°F. Season the tuna all over with kosher salt and black pepper. In a small bowl, combine the garlic and chile powder. Rub the mixture on the tuna and set aside while prepping the other ingredients.

2. In a 5- or 6-quart Dutch oven, melt the butter over medium heat. Cook, swirling occasionally, until the foam subsides, the milk solids turn golden brown, and it smells nutty and toasty, 2 to 4 minutes. (Watch carefully to see that it doesn't burn.)

3. Stir in the scallion whites and jalapeños and cook until tender and golden, 2 minutes. Add the corn, stirring occasionally, until lightly browned, 7 minutes. Stir in the tomatoes, the ½ teaspoon kosher salt, and a grind or two of black pepper. Nestle the tuna steaks into the pot and drizzle with the oil. Cover and bake until the vegetables are tender and the tuna is cooked to the desired doneness, 10 to 13 minutes for rare, 15 to 20 minutes for medium.

4. Taste the corn and add more kosher salt and a squeeze of lime, if needed. Serve topped with the scallion greens and flaky sea salt, with the lime wedges on the side.

SWAP IT OUT

Thick salmon fillets will work well here in place of the tuna.

VEG IT UP

You can add tender greens to the corn and tomatoes. Before serving, remove the tuna steaks from the pot and tent with foil to keep them warm. Add 4 to 5 ounces (4 to 5 cups) baby greens and stir over low heat until they wilt.

Saag Paneer

SERVES 4

2 tablespoons ghee or neutral oil, such as sunflower, grapeseed, or safflower, divided

8 ounces paneer, cut into 1-inch cubes

1 medium yellow onion, finely chopped

2 jalapeño or serrano chiles, seeded and diced

½ teaspoon kosher salt, plus more as needed

1 tablespoon grated fresh ginger

3 garlic cloves, minced or finely grated

1 teaspoon garam masala

½ teaspoon mustard seeds

½ teaspoon cumin seeds

1 pound (about 12 packed cups) mixed baby greens, such as any combination of spinach, chard, mustard greens, and kale, chopped

½ cup buttermilk (or use water)

⅓ cup heavy cream

Freshly ground black pepper

Indian pickle (such as lime, mango, or mixed vegetable), for serving (optional)

Plain yogurt, for serving (optional)

Saag paneer is a classic Indian recipe featuring silky, spiced leafy greens (such as spinach, mustard greens, or collards) studded with springy, creamy cubes of paneer cheese. This version takes those flavors but cooks them all in one pot. The key is sticking to baby greens, which don't need to be blanched first. You can chop the greens by hand or in a food processor—whatever is easier in your kitchen—but don't be tempted to throw them whole into the pot. They won't cook down as nicely. I like to brown the paneer until it's very dark; this helps it form a crisp crust and adds a caramelized flavor to the mix. You can serve this with rice or warm flatbread, if you like. And if you love pungent, funky condiments as much as I do, a big dollop of Indian pickle and some yogurt on the side makes this even better.

1. In a 5- or 6-quart Dutch oven, heat 1 tablespoon of the ghee over medium heat. When it shimmers, add the paneer in a single layer and cook until golden brown on both sides, flipping the cheese when it releases easily from the pot (about 7 minutes total). Transfer the paneer to a plate and tent foil on top to keep it warm.

2. To the pot, add the remaining 1 tablespoon ghee, the onion, and jalapeños, and season with a pinch of salt. Cook, stirring occasionally, until softened, 5 minutes. Stir in the ginger, garlic, garam masala, mustard seeds, and cumin seeds and cook until fragrant, 1 to 2 minutes.

3. Stir in the chopped greens, buttermilk, and the ½ teaspoon salt, and cook, stirring occasionally, until the greens are very tender and the liquid is absorbed, 8 to 10 minutes.

4. Remove from the heat and stir in the heavy cream and paneer. Season with salt and pepper to taste. Serve hot with Indian pickle and yogurt on the side, if you like.

SWAP IT OUT

If you can't find paneer, you can substitute another frying cheese, such as Halloumi, queso blanco, cheese curds, or Finnish bread cheese.

The Easiest Rice and Beans

with Quick Pickled Jalapeños

SERVES 4 TO 6

2 jalapeños, seeded if you like: 1 thinly sliced, 1 finely diced

1 lime, halved

1½ teaspoons kosher salt, plus more to taste

Large pinch of sugar (or use a drizzle of honey or agave syrup)

2 tablespoons extra-virgin olive oil

1 large red onion, chopped

1 small bunch fresh cilantro, leaves and tender stems separated and finely chopped

Freshly ground black pepper

4 garlic cloves, minced or finely grated

1 tablespoon tomato paste

2 teaspoons chili powder

1 teaspoon ground cumin (or coriander)

1 teaspoon dried oregano

2 cups vegetable stock or water

2 (15.5-ounce) cans black beans, drained and rinsed

1 cup long-grain white rice

Hot sauce, for serving (optional)

Cooking rice and beans in the same pot makes for one of the easiest and most adaptable meals around. Here it's perked up with homemade pickled jalapeños, which add heat and zip to the comforting, carbohydrate-y mix. You can use this basic recipe as a template, changing up the beans, the spices, and the cooking liquid (see Swap It Out). Just don't use brown rice, which needs more liquid and a much longer cooking time.

1. Place the sliced jalapeño in a small bowl and squeeze in enough lime juice to cover it (save the diced jalapeño for later). Add a pinch each of salt and sugar. Let sit at room temperature while you make the rice. (The jalapeños can be prepared up to 5 days ahead of time and stored in the refrigerator; they get softer and more pickled as they sit.)

2. In a 5- or 6-quart Dutch oven with a tight-fitting lid, heat the oil over medium-high heat. Add the onion, the diced jalapeño, cilantro stems, and a pinch each of salt and pepper, and sauté until tender, 3 to 4 minutes. Stir in the garlic, tomato paste, chili powder, cumin, and oregano, and cook until fragrant, 1 to 2 minutes.

3. Add the stock and bring to a boil. Stir in the beans, rice, and 1½ teaspoons salt and cover the pot. Reduce the heat to low and simmer, undisturbed, for 16 to 18 minutes, until the rice is tender.

4. Remove the pot from the heat, wrap a clean kitchen towel around the pot cover, re-cover the pot, and let it sit for 5 minutes to absorb some of the steam. Fluff the rice mixture with a fork and stir in the chopped cilantro leaves. Taste and season with salt as needed.

5. To serve, top each bowl of rice and beans with the pickled jalapeños, plus a drizzle of their pickling liquid. If the jalapeño is very mild, add a dash of hot sauce, if you like.

SWAP IT OUT

Substitute ½ cup salsa for an equal amount of the stock. Tangy salsa verde works really well here. To add a bright sweetness, try substituting ½ cup orange juice for some of the stock. Or use a cup of crushed tomatoes in place of a cup of stock. As long as you keep the ratio the same (1 cup rice to 2 cups liquid), the dish will work. Adding a bay leaf to the pot gives this a nice earthiness. Use any beans or a combination of beans; pinto and kidney are also delicious here.

ADD IT IN

If you want to add meat, you can use 2 to 4 ounces of diced bacon, chorizo or other sausages, or ground pork or turkey. Brown it in a little oil before adding it with the onion and diced jalapeño in Step 2.

SAVORY BREAD PUDDING
WITH ASPARAGUS, PESTO,
AND GRUYÈRE, PAGE 170

ROASTED CARROTS AND
BEETS WITH SMOKED
MOZZARELLA, DILL, AND
CRISPY BREAD CRUMBS,
PAGE 176

Casseroles

Garlicky Chicken

with Sugar Snap Peas, Pecorino, and Lemon

SERVES 3 OR 4

1½ pounds boneless, skinless chicken thighs

Kosher salt and freshly ground black pepper

1 lemon

4 garlic cloves: 2 finely grated, 2 thinly sliced

1 teaspoon Worcestershire sauce

3 tablespoons extra-virgin olive oil, plus more for drizzling

12 ounces sugar snap peas, trimmed

2 scallions, sliced (white and green parts separated)

3 fresh thyme sprigs

½ cup (2 ounces) grated pecorino Romano cheese, divided, plus more for serving

SWAP IT OUT

Broccolini, green beans, or thick asparagus stalks can replace the sugar snap peas. If you'd like to use white meat instead of thighs, choose chicken cutlets and layer them, overlapping slightly, over the peas, then start checking them after 15 minutes. They'll need less time to cook through.

The combination of lemon, garlic, and Worcestershire sauce gives this easy chicken dish a vaguely Caesar salad-like vibe but uses tender sugar snap peas for color and crunch in place of the usual romaine. Serve it with something—crusty bread, couscous, polenta—to catch all the garlicky, cheese-laden juices.

1. Heat the oven to 475°F. Season the chicken all over with salt and pepper and set aside.

2. Grate the lemon zest into a small bowl (save the naked lemon for later). Whisk in the grated garlic, Worcestershire sauce, a pinch of salt, and a grind of pepper. Whisk in the oil.

3. In a shallow 2-quart casserole or gratin dish, or an 11 × 7-inch baking dish, toss together the sugar snap peas with the scallion whites, thyme sprigs, sliced garlic, and a pinch of salt. Drizzle lightly with oil. Nestle the chicken into the peas. Spoon about half the garlic oil mixture over the chicken, stirring it up to make sure you get some of the solids in the bottom of the bowl. (Reserve the remaining garlic mixture for serving.) Sprinkle the chicken with ¼ cup of the pecorino.

4. Roast until the peas are tender and the chicken is browned on top and cooked through, 25 to 30 minutes.

5. Meanwhile, halve the lemon and squeeze the juice from half of it into the rest of the garlic oil. Whisk in the remaining ¼ cup pecorino. Taste and add more lemon juice and salt, if needed, to make it zippy and tangy.

6. Serve the chicken and peas drizzled with the dressing and sprinkled with the scallion greens and more pecorino, if you like.

Lemony Baked Rice

with Artichokes, White Beans,
and Caramelized Leeks

SERVES 4

3 leeks, white and light green
parts, halved lengthwise and
thinly sliced into half moons

5 tablespoons extra-virgin
olive oil

1½ teaspoons kosher salt,
divided, plus more to taste

½ teaspoon crushed red
pepper flakes

Freshly ground black pepper

1 lemon

1½ cups basmati rice, rinsed
and drained

1½ cups marinated artichokes,
drained and chopped

1 (15.5-ounce) can white
beans (such as cannellini or
Great Northern), drained and
rinsed

2½ cups boiling vegetable
stock or water

½ cup freshly grated
Parmesan cheese, plus more
for serving

½ cup thinly sliced or chopped
fresh basil, chives, mint, or
fennel fronds, plus more for
serving

Baking rice with loads of aromatics, vegetables, and beans
allows it to absorb maximum flavor with minimal fuss.
Here the rice is cooked with lemony leeks, white beans, and
marinated artichokes. Make sure to nibble on an artichoke
before adding them all to the pan. If it tastes too tart or
vinegary, give them a rinse before using. Brands vary a lot.
Those packed in extra-virgin olive oil tend to be the best.

1. Heat the oven to 400°F.

2. In a shallow 2-quart casserole or gratin dish, or an 11 × 7-inch
baking dish, combine the leeks, oil, ½ teaspoon of the salt, the
red pepper flakes, and a grind or two of black pepper. Grate
the zest from the lemon into the baking dish with the leeks and
toss well. Cut the naked lemon in half and set aside. Arrange
the leek mixture in an even layer and roast until it starts to
caramelize, about 25 minutes.

3. Sprinkle the rice evenly over the leeks, then top with the
artichokes, beans, and remaining 1 teaspoon salt. Add the
boiling stock, then seal the pan tightly with foil. Bake until the
rice is tender, 20 to 22 minutes.

4. Remove from the oven and let sit, covered, for 5 minutes.
Fluff the rice with a fork. Squeeze half the lemon over the rice,
then stir in the Parmesan and herbs. Season to taste with salt
and black pepper. Serve with the remaining lemon half, cut into
wedges, and more Parmesan and herbs, if you like.

SWAP IT OUT

If you can't get good
marinated artichokes,
sun-dried tomatoes make
a terrific substitute. Look
for oil-packed tomatoes,
then drain and dice them
up before adding.

Roasted Cod

with Buttery Potatoes and Anchovy

SERVES 4

1 lemon

12 oil-packed anchovy fillets, finely chopped

4 garlic cloves, minced or finely grated, divided

1¾ pounds Yukon Gold potatoes, peeled and sliced about ⅛ inch thick

4 scallions, thinly sliced (white and green parts separated)

¾ cup vegetable stock

4 fresh thyme sprigs

4 tablespoons (½ stick) unsalted butter, cut into ½-inch pieces, divided

1½ teaspoons kosher salt, divided, plus more to taste

¾ teaspoon freshly ground black pepper, divided, plus more to taste

4 (6- to 8-ounce) boneless, skinless cod fillets

¾ cup mayonnaise

1 tablespoon capers, drained and coarsely chopped

Rubbing a garlicky anchovy paste on pretty much any kind of fish before roasting is possibly my favorite way to add flavor without much work. Here, I use thick cod fillets, which are roasted on a bed of soft, thyme-infused potatoes, then served dolloped with caper mayonnaise. It's a dish that manages to be extremely comforting and zippy at the same time. Serve it with a spinach or lettuce salad (see page 244) if you're looking to add something green to the plate.

1. Heat the oven to 425°F. Grate the zest from the lemon into a small bowl, then stir in the anchovies and three-quarters of the garlic (save the remaining garlic for the mayo). Cut the naked lemon into wedges and set aside for serving.

2. In a shallow 2-quart casserole or gratin dish, or an 11 × 7-inch baking dish, combine the potatoes and scallion whites. Using a teaspoon, dollop about half of the anchovy mixture all over the potatoes, then add the stock and thyme to the dish. Scatter half of the butter pieces on top and sprinkle with ½ teaspoon of the salt and ¼ teaspoon of the pepper. Cover the dish with foil and bake until the potatoes are fork-tender, about 40 minutes.

3. While the potatoes are baking, season the cod all over with the remaining 1 teaspoon salt and ½ teaspoon pepper. Rub the reserved anchovy paste all over the fillets. Once the potatoes are soft, remove the baking dish from the oven and raise the temperature to 450°F. Place the fish on top of the potatoes and dot the fillets with the remaining butter pieces. Return to the oven and roast, uncovered, until the cod is opaque in the center and golden at the edges, 8 to 12 minutes.

4. While the fish roasts, make the caper sauce: In a small bowl, mix together the mayo, capers, remaining garlic, and salt and pepper to taste. Add a squeeze of lemon if it needs it.

5. To serve, squeeze a lemon wedge over the top of the cod and potatoes. Dollop caper sauce on the cod and garnish with the scallion greens and more lemon wedges on the side.

SWAP IT OUT

Salmon fillets will work perfectly well here in place of the cod.

Roasted Salmon Salad

with Limes and Chiles

SERVES 4

2 limes, halved

2 small fresh chiles or 1 large one, seeded if you like, thinly sliced

¼ cup thinly sliced red onion or shallot, divided

1½ tablespoons fish sauce, plus more to taste

Kosher salt

Pinch of sugar (or use a drop of honey), plus more to taste

¼ cup extra-virgin olive oil, plus more for drizzling

1¼ pounds salmon fillet, preferably one big, center-cut piece

8 cups salad greens, such as little gem, bibb, or Boston lettuce

1 cup mixed fresh soft herbs, such as cilantro, mint, and basil, leaves and tender stems

1 cup thinly sliced radishes or cucumbers (or both)

The juxtaposition of velvety salmon against crisp vegetables and a jumble of soft lettuces is just one of the joys of this tangy, summery salad. The other joy is the dressing, based on nuoc cham (a traditional Vietnamese dipping sauce), which has just enough fish sauce to give it depth and pungency but without overpowering the sweetness of the salmon. If you want to serve this with something extra on the side, plain white rice would be my first choice, followed by a crusty baguette.

1. Heat the oven to 350°F.

2. Squeeze the juice from one lime half into a small bowl. Add the chiles, half of the sliced onion (save the rest for serving), the fish sauce, and a pinch each salt and sugar. Let sit for 1 minute to dissolve the salt, then whisk in the oil. It won't emulsify, so mix it up again before using. Taste and add more sugar or fish sauce, if needed. Set aside.

3. Place the salmon into a shallow 2-quart casserole or gratin dish, or an 11 × 7-inch baking dish, sprinkle very lightly with salt, and drizzle generously with oil. Add the remaining 3 lime halves to the dish, surrounding the salmon. Roast until the fish is just cooked to taste, 10 to 20 minutes, depending upon the size and thickness of the pieces.

4. When the salmon is done, transfer it to a plate and spoon some of the dressing over it. Let it cool slightly, then break up the fish into large chunks.

5. Put the salad greens, remaining sliced onion, the herbs, and radishes or cucumber (or both) into a large shallow bowl or platter and add a little more of the dressing. Squeeze some of the juice from one of the roasted lime halves over it and drizzle with a little oil. Toss and taste, adding more lime juice, oil, or salt as needed.

6. Top with the salmon chunks and drizzle with more (or all) of the dressing. Serve with the 2 remaining roasted lime halves on the side for squeezing, if you like.

Creamy Corn and Polenta Bake

with Blue Cheese

SERVES 4 TO 6

2 tablespoons unsalted butter, cut into ½-inch pieces, plus more for the baking dish

4 cups vegetable or chicken stock

½ cup whole milk

1½ cups polenta (not instant) or coarse cornmeal

½ cup (2 ounces) grated Parmesan cheese, divided

1 teaspoon fine sea salt

1½ cups corn kernels, fresh (from 1 to 2 ears) or frozen

1½ cups quartered cherry tomatoes

4 ounces (about 1 cup) blue cheese, crumbled, plus more for garnish

½ cup fresh parsley leaves and tender stems, coarsely chopped, plus more for garnish

¼ cup fresh basil leaves, hand torn, plus more for garnish

1 scallion, thinly sliced

VEG IT UP

Stir 2 cups (2 ounces) of tender greens, like baby spinach, tatsoi, or arugula, into the polenta along with the corn kernels.

Baking polenta might take more time than simmering it on the stove, but it's almost entirely hands-off, and so much easier without all that stirring to worry about. Plus, if you've ever been singed by a rogue splash of molten polenta, you'll be happy to keep the simmering far from your forearms. In this recipe, the mild, nubby cornmeal is made even sweeter by the addition of plump, juicy corn kernels—either fresh or frozen—and some quartered cherry tomatoes. Then the combination of blue cheese and Parmesan rounds it all out with a welcome savory, salty jolt.

1. Put an oven rack in the upper third of your oven and heat to 350°F. Generously butter a shallow 2-quart casserole or gratin dish, or an 11 × 7-inch baking dish.

2. Pour the stock and milk into the casserole dish, then stir in the polenta, ¼ cup of the Parmesan, and the salt. Bake, uncovered, for 30 minutes, then give everything a good stir (don't worry if the mixture looks separated at this point). Continue to bake until the polenta thickens somewhat and comes together, 20 to 25 minutes longer.

3. Stir in the corn, tomatoes, blue cheese, parsley, basil, and scallion. Bake for another 10 to 15 minutes, until very thick and creamy.

4. Turn the broiler on high. Sprinkle the remaining ¼ cup Parmesan all over the surface of the polenta and scatter on the butter pieces. Broil until the cheese starts to bubble and develop brown spots all over, 2 to 4 minutes (watch carefully so it doesn't blacken).

5. Remove from the oven and let the polenta stand for about 10 minutes before serving. Spoon polenta into individual bowls and sprinkle with more blue cheese, parsley, and basil.

VEGAN UPGRADE

Skip the Parmesan. If you
like, you can sprinkle some
nutritional yeast on top after
the dish is out of the broiler.

Roasted Mushrooms

with Crispy Polenta and Parmesan

SERVES 3 OR 4

12 ounces mushrooms, such as maitake, cremini, white button, shiitake, or oyster, cut into 1-inch chunks (about 5 cups)

4 tablespoons extra-virgin olive oil, divided

4 large fresh thyme sprigs

3 garlic cloves, thinly sliced

2 shallots, thinly sliced

Kosher salt and freshly ground black pepper

1 pound precooked polenta, cut into 1-inch chunks (about 3 cups)

⅓ cup grated Parmesan cheese, plus more for serving

⅓ cup chopped fresh parsley leaves and tender stems, for garnish

Crushed red pepper flakes, for serving (optional)

Using precooked polenta makes this dish an absolute breeze, and perfect for a busy night when you're looking for something meatless, comforting, and different from, say, your go-to pasta. Here, the mushrooms and polenta are seasoned with thyme, garlic, and shallots, then roasted until golden under a shower of savory Parmesan cheese. You can use whatever mushrooms you like. I especially love maitake, which have a lacy shape that gets crispy at the edges. Or use a combination of mushrooms for a variety of flavors and textures. With the mushrooms, polenta, and cheese, you can't go wrong.

1. Heat the oven to 450°F. In a shallow 2-quart casserole or gratin dish, or an 11 × 7-inch baking dish, combine the mushrooms, 3 tablespoons of the oil, the thyme, garlic, shallots, ½ teaspoon salt, and a few grinds of black pepper, tossing well. Roast for 15 minutes; the mushrooms should have started to wilt and glisten.

2. While the mushrooms are roasting, in a large bowl, toss the polenta with the remaining 1 tablespoon oil, a big pinch or two of salt, and a few grinds of black pepper. Take the baking dish out of the oven and stir in the polenta. Sprinkle the Parmesan over the top and bake for another 15 to 20 minutes, until the mushrooms are tender.

3. Turn on the broiler, and broil for 1 to 2 minutes, until the top of the polenta is crispy with some brown spots.

4. To serve, garnish with parsley and finish with more Parmesan and red pepper flakes, if you like.

Puffy Spoonbread

with Corn, Crab, and Roasted Red Peppers

SERVES 6 TO 8

4 tablespoons (½ stick) unsalted butter, melted and cooled, plus more for the baking dish

1 cup fine cornmeal

1¼ teaspoons kosher salt

½ cup boiling water

1½ cups buttermilk

4 large eggs

2¼ teaspoons baking powder

1 cup corn kernels, fresh (from 1 large ear) or frozen and thawed

8 ounces crabmeat, preferably jumbo lump

½ cup roasted red peppers, diced

¼ cup chopped fresh cilantro leaves and tender stems

4 scallions, thinly sliced, divided

Tabasco sauce, for serving

Lemon wedges, for serving

This luscious, fluffy Southern dish is like a cross between corn bread and a billowing soufflé, with a golden top and soft, creamy center that's slightly sweet from the fresh (or frozen) corn. The crabmeat definitely takes it up a notch, transforming it from a side dish to the centerpiece of an elegant brunch or a light dinner.

1. Heat the oven to 350°F and generously butter a shallow 2-quart casserole or gratin dish, or an 11 × 7-inch baking dish.

2. In a large bowl, combine the cornmeal and salt. Whisk in the boiling water and break up any lumps. Let cool for 5 minutes. Add the buttermilk, melted butter, and the eggs, one at a time, beating well between additions, and whisk until smooth. Add the baking powder until combined.

3. Fold in the corn, crabmeat, red peppers, cilantro, and three-quarters of the scallions, saving the rest for garnish. Scape the batter into the prepared baking dish and bake until golden brown and a toothpick inserted into the center comes out clean, 50 to 60 minutes, rotating the baking dish halfway through.

4. Let stand for at least 10 minutes before serving. Serve hot or warm, garnished with the remaining scallions and with Tabasco sauce and lemon wedges on the side.

SWAP IT OUT

You can substitute cooked shrimp for the crabmeat. Use 8 ounces diced cooked shrimp and add it instead of the crabmeat in Step 3.

VEGETARIAN UPGRADE

You can substitute grated cheddar cheese for the crabmeat. Use 6 ounces (1½ cups), adding 1 cup in Step 3 with the corn, and sprinkling the remaining ½ cup on top of the batter just before baking.

Cheddar Soufflé

with Prosciutto and Arugula

1 tablespoon extra-virgin olive oil, plus more as needed

5 ounces (5 cups) arugula, coarsely chopped, plus more for serving

½ cup chopped green olives or oil-packed sun-dried tomatoes

Kosher salt and freshly ground black pepper

9 large eggs

2 ounces prosciutto, chopped (½ cup)

6 scallions, thinly sliced

5 garlic cloves, minced or finely grated

1 pound (4 cups) grated sharp cheddar cheese

½ teaspoon freshly grated nutmeg

Tabasco sauce, as needed

Flaky sea salt, for serving

This puffy soufflé is a bit like a crustless quiche in texture, and loaded with punchy, salty flavors from the olives, prosciutto, and a generous amount of garlic. The cheddar cheese makes it creamy, and arugula balances the richness of the dish, lending a pleasing edge of bitterness to the mix. If you can find wild arugula, its herbal, mineral flavor will work beautifully here. Serve this soufflé for a light dinner or for brunch, with more arugula on the side.

1. Heat the oven to 350°F and brush a shallow 2-quart casserole or gratin dish, or an 11 × 7-inch baking dish with oil.

2. Add the arugula, olives, a pinch of kosher salt, and a little pepper to the casserole dish. Drizzle with 1 tablespoon oil and toss to combine. Bake until the arugula wilts and softens, about 10 minutes.

3. Meanwhile, in a large bowl, whisk the eggs until frothy. Whisk in the prosciutto, scallions, garlic, cheddar, nutmeg, ¼ teaspoon pepper, and 2 dashes of Tabasco. Pour the mixture into the casserole dish and gently stir to combine it with the arugula. Smooth the surface with a spatula.

4. Bake until the top is golden brown and puffed, and the eggs are set, 40 to 45 minutes. Transfer to a wire rack and let cool slightly. Cut the soufflé into squares and serve warm or at room temperature, topped with flaky sea salt and more Tabasco, if you like, and with arugula on the side, drizzled with a little more oil.

SWAP IT OUT

If you don't have prosciutto, you can use another salty cured meat, like ham, cured sausage or salami, or cooked bacon or pancetta.

VEGETARIAN UPGRADE

You can skip the prosciutto and stir in 1 cup diced marinated artichokes instead. Or, leave out the meat and just increase the olives or sun-dried tomatoes to 1 cup total—or use ½ cup each.

Savory Bread Pudding

with Asparagus, Pesto, and Gruyère

SERVES 6

2¼ cups whole milk

6 large eggs

1 teaspoon kosher salt, divided

¼ teaspoon freshly ground black pepper

1 large baguette (10 to 12 ounces), preferably day old, cut into 1-inch chunks

½ tablespoon unsalted butter, plus more for greasing the foil

1 large bunch (1¼ pounds) asparagus, trimmed and cut into 1½-inch pieces

1 tablespoon extra-virgin olive oil

1 cup (4 ounces) grated Gruyère (or use Swiss cheese)

½ cup prepared pesto, store-bought or homemade

SWAP IT OUT

Sugar snap peas make a great substitute for the asparagus. Halve about 8 ounces of them crosswise, then continue with the recipe. You might have to roast them for a few minutes longer; they're done when they are just tender and bright green.

VEG IT UP

Add ½ cup halved or quartered cherry tomatoes along with the pesto in Step 5.

Like a puffy soufflé with golden brown edges, this savory bread pudding has the same cozy appeal as mac and cheese but is much more elegant and perfect for spring, thanks to nuggets of asparagus layered in with the baguette. Serve it warm or at room temperature, for dinner or for brunch. And if you're feeling particularly decadent, leftovers can be sliced and fried in butter to crisp the edges.

1. Heat the oven to 400°F. In a large bowl, whisk together the milk, eggs, ½ teaspoon of the salt, and the pepper. Gently toss in the bread chunks, and let it sit while you prepare the remaining ingredients, stirring occasionally.

2. Butter one side of a piece of foil large enough to cover your casserole dish and set it aside.

3. In a shallow 2-quart casserole or gratin dish, or an 11 × 7-inch baking dish, toss together the asparagus, oil, and remaining ½ teaspoon salt. Roast until the asparagus is cooked through but still firm, about 10 minutes, tossing halfway through. Remove the casserole dish from the oven and, using tongs, carefully transfer half the asparagus to a plate to cool slightly.

4. Add the butter to the asparagus left in the hot casserole dish and swirl it around to coat the bottom of the dish. Scoop half of the soaked bread into the dish and mix it with the asparagus, arranging everything in one layer.

5. Top the bread with half the Gruyère and dot with half the pesto. Mix the asparagus from the plate into the bowl with the remaining soaked bread, then spread this mixture on top of the pesto. Sprinkle with the remaining Gruyère. Cover the dish with the prepared foil, buttered side down.

6. Bake for 30 minutes, then remove the foil. Continue to bake until golden on the edges and springy in the middle, about 15 minutes. (If you'd like, broil on low for 1 to 2 minutes for a more browned top.) Let cool for about 5 minutes, then dollop with the remaining pesto and serve.

Acorn Squash

with Taleggio, Honey, and Aleppo Almonds

SERVES 4

1 acorn squash (about 2 pounds), halved lengthwise, seeded, and cut into 1-inch wedges (no need to peel)

3 fresh thyme sprigs

3 tablespoons extra-virgin olive oil, plus more for drizzling

2 tablespoons plus 1 teaspoon good dark honey, such as buckwheat or chestnut, divided

¾ teaspoon kosher salt, plus more as needed

Freshly cracked black pepper

1 large shallot, thinly sliced

4 teaspoons balsamic vinegar, plus more for drizzling

6 ounces soft cow's milk cheese with washed rind, such as taleggio, fontina, or Brie, hand torn into small pieces (including rind)

⅓ cup coarsely chopped toasted, salted almonds

½ teaspoon Aleppo pepper or Turkish pepper, such as Urfa, plus more as needed

1 lemon

Flaky sea salt

Bitter lettuces, such as arugula, radicchio, or frisée, or use baby lettuces instead

If I didn't have a family to feed, I'd happily eat roasted vegetables topped with melted cheese pretty much every day (see Caramelized Carrots with Pancetta, Olives, and Crispy Parmesan on page 50 and Roasted Carrots and Beets with Smoked Mozzarella, Dill, and Crispy Bread Crumbs on page 176 for further evidence). Here, the vegetable in question is acorn squash, sliced into golden crescents and topped with a gooey layer of washed-rind cheese. Chopped almonds provide some crunch, smoky chile flakes give a bit of heat, and a drizzle of amber honey adds a contrasting sweet note. Then, just before serving, I plop the whole thing down on a bed of bitter lettuces and quick-pickled shallots for verve. Who needs anything else?

1. Heat the oven to 400°F. Place squash and thyme sprigs in a shallow 2-quart casserole dish or an 11 × 7-inch baking dish.

2. In a small bowl, whisk together the oil, 2 tablespoons of the honey, the kosher salt, and a pinch of black pepper. Pour over the squash and toss to combine. Arrange the squash wedges so they are standing up like boats, with the skin side down (don't worry if some fall over, it's inevitable). Roast until the squash is soft and caramelized, 45 to 50 minutes.

3. Meanwhile, **make the pickled shallots:** In the same small bowl you just used (no need to wash it), combine the shallot, balsamic vinegar, remaining 1 teaspoon honey, and a pinch of kosher salt, and set aside for at least 30 minutes.

4. Once the squash is golden and tender, sprinkle the cheese onto the wedges (it's okay if some cheese falls onto the baking dish). Sprinkle the squash with the almonds and Aleppo pepper, then grate the zest from half the lemon (or the whole lemon if yours is small) directly on top of everything. Bake until the cheese is melted, about 5 minutes.

5. Cut the naked lemon into quarters. When the squash is done, squeeze the juice from a lemon wedge all over it, then drizzle with balsamic vinegar and oil, and season with more Aleppo pepper, if you like, and flaky sea salt.

6. Serve the squash with lemon wedges, lettuces, and pickled shallots alongside and drizzled with more vinegar and oil.

SWAP IT OUT

Other winter squash varieties can stand in for the acorn squash. Just slice them up (peeled or not, as you like), and then check on them often while they are roasting, since different varieties may need more or less time in the oven. Sweet potatoes, cut lengthwise into wedges, would also work well.

Roasted Carrots and Beets

with Smoked Mozzarella, Dill, and Crispy Bread Crumbs

SERVES 4

1 pound **carrots**, peeled and sliced into ½-inch coins

1 pound **beets**, peeled and cut into ½-inch wedges

¾ cup **vegetable or chicken stock**, plus more if needed

1 teaspoon **coriander seeds**, cracked with the flat side of a knife or with a mortar and pestle

1¼ teaspoons **kosher salt**, divided

Freshly cracked black pepper

2 fat **garlic cloves**, smashed and peeled

5 tablespoons **extra-virgin olive oil**, divided

1 cup **panko bread crumbs**

1½ cups (6 ounces) **smoked mozzarella**, hand pulled into small pieces

Lemon wedges, for serving

½ cup **fresh dill** (or use **mint or parsley**), coarsely chopped

Flaky sea salt, for serving

SWAP IT OUT

Other root veggies will work well here, including sweet potatoes, turnips, celery root, and radishes.

I like to make this in the dead of winter, when root vegetables are pretty much the only viable options at the farmers' market and I'm desperate for a little color on the table. In varying shades of magenta and bright orange, the carrots and beets are baked until very tender, then topped with puddles of melted smoked mozzarella, crispy, garlicky bread crumbs, and lots of fresh herbs. The veggies balance out all the gooey cheese while the herbs, garlic, and a big squirt of lemon at the end add just the right level of spunkiness. It makes a light, meatless meal on its own, or may be served as a spectacular side dish to a simple roast chicken or fish. Note that the beets are peeled before roasting. It's a slightly unusual technique that works really well here.

1. Heat the oven to 400°F.

2. In a shallow 2-quart casserole or gratin dish, or an 11 × 7-inch baking dish, combine the carrots, beets, stock, cracked coriander seeds, 1 teaspoon of the kosher salt, and ½ teaspoon pepper, and toss until well combined. Place the garlic on top of the vegetables (sitting above the liquid in the pan) and drizzle everything with 2 tablespoons of the oil. Cover the dish with foil and roast for 1 hour. Uncover the dish and continue to bake, uncovered, for another 20 to 30 minutes, until the veggies are tender when pierced with a fork.

3. Remove the pan from the oven and raise the oven temperature to 450°F.

4. Pluck the garlic out of the pan. On a cutting board, using the flat side of a chef's knife, smush the soft roasted garlic into a paste. Put the paste into a small bowl and stir in the bread crumbs, remaining 3 tablespoons oil, remaining ¼ teaspoon kosher salt, and a pinch of pepper. Toss until well combined.

5. Sprinkle the mozzarella all over the carrots and beets, then top with the seasoned bread crumbs. Roast until golden brown, 10 to 14 minutes. Squeeze a lemon wedge all over the top of the casserole. Serve sprinkled with dill and flaky sea salt, with more lemon wedges on the side.

Soup Pots

SPICED CHICKEN AND
COUSCOUS SOUP WITH
VEGETABLES, PAGE 181

Spiced Chicken and Couscous Soup

with Vegetables

SERVES 4 TO 6

3 tablespoons extra-virgin olive oil, plus more as needed

2 leeks, white and light green parts, halved lengthwise and thinly sliced into half moons

1 teaspoon kosher salt, plus more as needed

1 bunch fresh cilantro, stems and leaves separated and chopped

3 garlic cloves, finely chopped

1 tablespoon tomato paste

2 teaspoons baharat or garam masala

½ cinnamon stick (about 1 inch)

1 pound boneless, skinless chicken thighs, cut into ¾-inch pieces

2 celery stalks or carrots, diced (or use both celery and carrots if you like)

1 small fennel bulb, diced

1 cup peeled and diced turnip or rutabaga

6 cups chicken or vegetable stock, plus more as needed

Freshly ground black pepper

1 cup pearl couscous

Lime wedges, for serving

Urfa or Aleppo pepper, or hot paprika, for serving

In this complex, vegetable-rich chicken soup, an aromatic spice blend—either baharat or garam masala—adds a heady fragrance to the pot while the combination of cinnamon and tomato paste lends a subtle sweetness. You can make this as light and thin or as thick and hearty as you like; just keep adding stock or water until it's the chicken soup of your dreams—sustaining, comforting, and profoundly flavorful.

1. In a large soup pot, heat the oil over medium-high heat. Add the leeks and a pinch of salt and sauté until they begin to brown, 7 to 10 minutes.

2. Stir the cilantro stems into the pot along with the garlic (save the cilantro leaves for later). Cook for 1 to 2 minutes, until fragrant. Stir in the tomato paste, baharat, and the cinnamon stick and cook until the paste begins to caramelize, 1 to 2 minutes.

3. If the pot looks dry, drizzle in a little more oil. Stir in the chicken and a pinch of salt and sauté until the chicken starts to brown, about 3 minutes. Stir in the celery, fennel, turnip, and another pinch of salt and sauté until the vegetables start to wilt, 3 to 5 minutes. Add the stock, 1 teaspoon salt, and a generous amount of black pepper. Bring to a boil, then reduce the heat to medium-low and simmer, uncovered, until the vegetables are nearly soft, 20 to 30 minutes.

4. Stir in the couscous and continue to simmer until it is tender, 8 to 10 minutes longer.

5. Taste and add a squeeze of lime juice and more salt, if needed. If the soup needs thinning out, stir in some more stock or water. Stir in the cilantro leaves and serve bowls of the soup topped with the Urfa pepper and lime wedges on the side for more squeezing.

VEG IT UP

This soup is a perfect place to add greens. Stir 4 to 5 ounces (4 to 5 cups) baby greens into the pot with the couscous in Step 4.

Lemony Turkey and White Bean Soup

with Winter Greens

SERVES 4

3 tablespoons extra-virgin olive oil, plus more for serving

1 large onion, diced

1 large carrot, diced

1 bunch sturdy greens, such as kale, broccoli rabe, mustard greens, or collards

1 tablespoon tomato paste

¾ teaspoon ground cumin, plus more to taste

⅛ teaspoon crushed red pepper flakes, plus more to taste

½ pound ground turkey

3 garlic cloves, minced

1 tablespoon finely grated fresh ginger

1 teaspoon kosher salt, plus more to taste

2 (15.5-ounce) cans white beans, drained and rinsed

4 to 6 cups chicken stock, homemade (page 247) or store-bought

1 cup chopped soft fresh herbs, such as parsley, mint, dill, basil, tarragon, chives, or a combination

Fresh lemon juice, to taste

This herby, piquant soup can be as hearty or brothy as you like. To make it thicker, use a spoon to crush some of the beans against the side of the pot; this releases their starch. Or for a thinner, lighter version, add more stock or water and leave the beans intact. Either way, it's a bone-warming meal full of beans and plenty of vegetables, rounded out with just a little meat.

1. Heat a large pot over medium-high heat for a minute or so to warm it up, then add the oil and heat until it thins out, about 30 seconds. Add the onion and carrot and sauté until very soft and brown at the edges, 7 to 10 minutes.

2. Meanwhile, rinse the greens and pull the leaves off the stems. Tear or chop the leaves into bite-size pieces and set aside.

3. When the onion is golden, add the tomato paste, cumin, and red pepper flakes to the pot and sauté until the paste darkens, about 1 minute. Add the turkey, garlic, ginger, and salt, and sauté, breaking up the meat with your spoon, until the turkey is browned in spots, 4 to 7 minutes.

4. Add the beans and enough stock to cover everything and bring to a simmer. Simmer until the soup is thick and flavorful, adding more salt, if needed, 15 to 25 minutes. If you like a thicker broth, you can smash up some of the beans with the back of the spoon to release their starch. Or leave the beans whole for a brothier soup.

5. Add the greens to the pot and simmer until they are very soft. This will take 5 to 10 minutes for most greens, but tough collard greens might take 15 minutes (add a little water if the broth gets too reduced).

6. Stir the herbs and lemon juice into the pot, taste, and add more salt, cumin, and lemon juice until the broth is lively and bright tasting. Serve topped with a drizzle of oil and more red pepper flakes, if desired.

SWAP IT OUT

Using ground pork in place of turkey makes this richer. Using ground chicken makes it lighter and sweeter.

VEG IT UP

There's room in the pot for even more vegetables. You can double the greens and/ or add a cup or two of diced fresh or canned tomatoes.

VEGAN UPGRADE

Substitute vegetable stock for the chicken stock, and 10 ounces chopped mushrooms for the ground turkey, sautéing them with the ginger in Step 3.

Kimchi Pork Soup

with Napa Cabbage and Silken Tofu

SERVES 4 TO 6

3 tablespoons neutral oil, such as grapeseed, sunflower, or safflower

1 medium onion, diced

1¼ teaspoons kosher salt, divided

1 pound ground pork

¼ teaspoon freshly ground black pepper

3 garlic cloves, grated or minced

1 teaspoon gochugaru or ¼ teaspoon cayenne

1 tablespoon gochujang (or substitute another chile paste, such as Sriracha or sambal oelek)

6 cups coarsely chopped napa or green cabbage (from ½ small head, about 14 ounces)

1½ cups kimchi, squeezed dry and chopped (reserve juices)

1 to 2 teaspoons sugar or honey, or to taste (optional)

6 cups chicken or vegetable stock

1 to 2 tablespoons fish sauce, or to taste

1 (14- to 16-ounce) package silken or soft tofu, cut into cubes

Toasted sesame oil, for serving (optional)

Sliced scallion greens, for serving

With a zingy, chile-flecked broth full of cabbage, tofu, and some ground pork for flavor, this soup was inspired by the deep, spicy complexity of a Korean kimchi jjigae, or kimchi stew. If you can, seek out a kimchi that's been aged. Fresh kimchi is milder, and while it will work, aged kimchi will give you the deepest, sour-funky flavor that makes this dish so beloved and distinct. This recipe also calls for gochujang (a mildly sweet Korean chile paste) and gochugaru (spicy Korean chile flakes). If you can't find them, you can use one of the substitutes listed. But if you love heat and spice, they're worth keeping on hand to use in marinades, sauces, braises, and as fiery garnishes, and are easily available online if they are not at your local market.

1. In a soup pot, heat the neutral oil over medium-high heat. Add the onion and ¼ teaspoon of the salt and cook, stirring frequently, until it is lightly browned, 5 to 8 minutes.

2. To the pot, add the pork, the remaining 1 teaspoon salt, and the pepper, and cook, breaking up the pork with a metal spoon, until it is no longer pink, about 5 minutes. Add the garlic, gochugaru, and gochujang and sauté for 1 minute.

3. Add the cabbage to the pot along with the kimchi and reserved juices, and sugar, if using, and cook 1 minute longer. Add the stock and fish sauce and bring to a simmer. Cover and cook for 10 minutes, then taste and add more fish sauce, if needed.

4. Lay the tofu in the soup, and simmer until it is warmed through, about 3 minutes. Serve with a drizzle of sesame oil (if using) and scallion greens on top.

VEGAN UPGRADE

This is excellent when made with mushrooms instead of pork. Sauté 8 ounces chopped shiitake mushrooms in Step 2 instead of the pork, letting them get very brown. Then substitute either coconut aminos or more soy sauce for the fish sauce.

Crispy Bacon, Bean, and Kale Soup

SERVES 4 TO 6

½ pound **bacon**, diced

2 large **white onions**, finely chopped

2 **celery stalks**, finely chopped

2 **carrots**, thinly sliced

1 **bay leaf**

1 teaspoon **kosher salt**, plus more as needed

Freshly ground **black pepper**

4 **garlic cloves**, minced

1 large **jalapeño**, seeded if you like, chopped

1 tablespoon **tomato paste**

6 cups **chicken or vegetable stock**

2 (15.5-ounce) cans **beans** (any kind you like), drained and rinsed

1 large bunch (8 ounces) **kale**, stems removed, leaves thinly sliced

¼ cup **fresh parsley leaves and tender stems**, chopped

1 teaspoon **apple cider vinegar**, plus more to taste

Hot sauce (optional)

Avocado slices, sour cream, or Greek yogurt (optional)

Use whatever kind of canned beans you've got to make this easy, relatively speedy soup. The bacon does the heavy lifting, adding richness and tons of flavor that the beans and vegetables will handily soak up. Don't stint on the vinegar at the end, as the soup will need the brightness. I love to serve this with sliced avocado to add creaminess, but a dollop of sour cream or yogurt would work, too, if you don't have a nice ripe avocado at the ready.

1. In a large pot over medium heat, cook the bacon, stirring occasionally, until golden brown and crispy, 8 to 10 minutes. Use a slotted spoon to transfer the bacon to a plate, leaving the fat in the pan.

2. Raise the heat to medium-high and add the onions, celery, carrots, bay leaf, and a big pinch each of salt and pepper; cook until lightly browned, 8 to 10 minutes, stirring frequently (add a little water, if necessary, to prevent burning on the bottom of the pot). Stir in the garlic and jalapeño and cook until fragrant, 2 minutes longer. Stir in the tomato paste and cook until it darkens, 1 minute longer.

3. Add the stock, beans, kale, and 1 teaspoon salt. Bring to a boil, then reduce the heat and simmer for 25 to 35 minutes, stirring occasionally, until the carrots are soft. Remove the bay leaf and stir in the parsley and vinegar. Taste and add more vinegar and salt to taste. Serve topped with the bacon, and hot sauce and avocado (or sour cream or yogurt), if you like.

VEG IT UP

Add more greens; this soup can take it! Just double the kale or add some other greens along with it, like spinach, cabbage, collard greens, or mustard greens.

Coconut Fish Curry

with Shiitakes and Snow Peas

SERVES 4

1 pound flaky white fish fillets
(such as hake, cod, or halibut),
cut into 1-inch cubes

½ teaspoon kosher salt, plus
more as needed

2 tablespoons coconut oil
(or peanut or safflower oil)

2 shallots or 1 small onion,
minced

1 Thai or serrano chile,
seeded and thinly sliced

4 tablespoons chopped fresh
cilantro, stems and leaves
separated

1 tablespoon minced fresh
ginger

2 garlic cloves, minced

4 ounces shiitake mushroom
caps, sliced ¼ inch thick

8 ounces snow peas, cut into
1-inch pieces

3 tablespoons prepared Thai
red curry paste

1 cup unsweetened full-fat
coconut milk

2 teaspoons fish sauce, plus
more as needed

Zest and juice of 1 lime

Thai red curry paste is one of those genius ingredients that allows you to add depth and savory richness to dishes without much more effort than unearthing that tiny jar from the back of the fridge (pro tip: keep it on the door for easy access). Here, it gives pungency and spice to sweet coconut milk, which is simmered into a silky, gingery sauce for fish and vegetables. Bowls of rice or rice noodles would round this out nicely.

1. Pat the fish dry all over with paper towels and season lightly with salt; set aside.

2. In a large pot, heat the oil over medium-high heat. Add the shallots, chile, and cilantro stems and sauté until tender and browned at the edges, about 5 minutes. Stir in the ginger and garlic and continue to sauté until fragrant, about 1 minute longer.

3. Add the mushrooms and snow peas to the pot and sauté until golden brown and tender, about 5 minutes. Season with the ½ teaspoon salt. Stir in the curry paste and cook 2 minutes.

4. Pour in the coconut milk, scraping up any curry paste with a wooden spoon. Add the fish sauce, lime zest, and lime juice and bring to a simmer. Add the fish cubes and simmer until the sauce thickens slightly and the fish is cooked through, 5 to 7 minutes, stirring occasionally. Taste and add more salt and/or fish sauce, if needed.

5. Serve with a scattering of torn cilantro leaves on top.

SWAP IT OUT

This curry is so adaptable; you can use pretty much any quick-cooking vegetables instead of mushrooms and snow peas, in any combination that sounds good to you. Try sliced sugar snap peas, halved green beans, diced tomatoes, diced zucchini or summer squash, thinly sliced fennel, corn, or chopped greens like kale, spinach, or chard. And 1 pound of large shrimp or cubed boneless chicken can be substituted for the fish. Just reduce the cooking time for the shrimp (usually 3 or 4 minutes will do it), or increase it for the chicken (10 to 15 minutes).

VEGAN UPGRADE

Substitute firm tofu for the fish. And instead of fish sauce, season the curry to taste with soy sauce and toasted sesame oil. It will give you a slightly different flavor profile from the original dish, but it's just as compelling.

Cauliflower-Carrot Soup

with Smoky Paprika Shrimp

SERVES 6 TO 8

1 pound extra-large shrimp, peeled and deveined

5 tablespoons extra-virgin olive oil, divided, plus more for serving

2 teaspoons smoked paprika, divided

2¼ teaspoons kosher salt, divided, plus more as needed

1½ teaspoons ground coriander, divided

Freshly ground black pepper

3 tablespoons fresh lime juice, divided, plus more to taste

1 large white onion, diced (2 cups)

2 large garlic cloves, finely chopped

4 medium carrots (12 ounces), cut into ½-inch pieces

3 tablespoons red or white miso paste

2 pounds cauliflower, trimmed and cut into florets (8 cups)

1 teaspoon finely grated lime zest

Smoky chile powder, for serving

Flaky sea salt, for serving

Fresh cilantro leaves, for serving

Even without the smoky pink shrimp floating in each bowl, this gently spiced vegetable purée makes for a quietly delightful meal, with its warming blend of lime and miso adding brightness and depth to the cauliflower and carrots. But the shrimp really make it shine, and they only take about 5 minutes to sauté. Like most puréed vegetable soups, this one is highly adaptable. See Swap It Out for some ideas, and feel free to make this your own.

1. In a medium bowl, combine the shrimp with 1 tablespoon of the oil, 1 teaspoon of the paprika, ¾ teaspoon of the kosher salt, ½ teaspoon of the coriander, and a lot of pepper, tossing well.

2. In a large soup pot, heat 2 tablespoons of the oil over medium-high heat. Add the shrimp and cook for 1 to 2 minutes on each side, turning as they start to become pink. Transfer the cooked shrimp to a bowl and toss with 1 tablespoon of the lime juice. Set aside until serving time.

3. Return the (uncleaned) pot to medium heat. Add the remaining 2 tablespoons oil and heat until the oil warms and thins out, about 30 seconds. Stir in the onion and cook, stirring occasionally, until soft and lightly colored, 7 to 10 minutes. Stir in the garlic, remaining 1 teaspoon paprika, and remaining 1 teaspoon coriander; cook until fragrant, 30 seconds to 1 minute.

4. Add the carrots, remaining 1½ teaspoons kosher salt, and 6 cups water to the pot. Stir in the miso until it dissolves. Bring the mixture to a simmer and cook, uncovered, for 8 minutes. Stir in the cauliflower and cook, covered, over medium-low heat until the vegetables are very tender, 20 to 30 minutes.

(recipe continues)

5. Remove the soup pot from the heat. Using an immersion blender, purée the soup until smooth. (Alternatively, you can let the soup cool slightly, then purée it in batches in a food processor or blender.)

6. Add the shrimp to the puréed soup, return the pot to medium heat, and cook just until the shrimp are warmed through. Stir in the lime zest and the remaining 2 tablespoons lime juice just before serving; taste and add more lime juice, if needed. Ladle the soup into individual bowls, drizzle with oil, and sprinkle with chile powder, flaky sea salt, and cilantro leaves.

SWAP IT OUT

Substitute ½-inch chunks of boneless chicken or turkey for the shrimp, making sure to cook the meat through (3 to 6 minutes) before transferring it to a plate. Other vegetables can be substituted for the cauliflower and carrots. Try potatoes, winter squash, broccoli, turnips, celery root, fennel, or a combination.

VEG IT UP

Stir 2 to 3 cups (2 to 3 ounces) of baby spinach, kale, or other greens into the soup pot before adding the cooked shrimp. Cook until the greens wilt, then stir in the shrimp.

VEGAN UPGRADE

Leave the shrimp out entirely; it's just as good without it.

Crispy Chickpea Stew

with Greens, Lemon, and Feta

SERVES 4 TO 6

3 (15.5-ounce) cans chickpeas, drained and rinsed, divided

1 large lemon

4 tablespoons extra-virgin olive oil, divided, plus more for serving

1¼ teaspoons kosher salt, divided, plus more as needed

Freshly ground black pepper

6 garlic cloves: 2 thinly sliced, 4 minced

1 large onion, diced

1 tablespoon fresh oregano, finely chopped

Pinch of crushed red pepper flakes, plus more for serving

12 ounces hardy winter greens, such as collards, kale, or mustard greens, stems removed and coarsely chopped

4 cups vegetable or chicken stock

1 cup (8 ounces) crumbled feta or goat cheese

¼ cup fresh parsley leaves, for serving

VEG IT UP

Juicy halved cherry tomatoes are great here; add 1 or 2 cups of them along with the feta.

The hardest part about making this dish is not eating all the garlic-strewn crispy chickpeas right after you've made them. But try to resist—they will taste even better as a crunchy topping to this gorgeous, velvety stew laden with tender greens, salty feta cheese, and even more chickpeas. All the textures here make this dish highly appealing and very hard to stop eating. You've been warned.

1. Place 2 cups of the drained chickpeas on a clean kitchen towel or a double layer of paper towels and pat them dry. Grate the zest from the lemon into a small bowl and cut the naked lemon in half. Set both aside.

2. In a large soup pot, heat 1 tablespoon of the oil over medium-high heat. Add the towel-dried chickpeas, ½ teaspoon of the salt, and a grind or two of black pepper and cook, stirring occasionally, until crisped, 8 to 10 minutes. Add another 1 tablespoon of the oil and the sliced garlic to the pot (save the minced garlic for later). Cook until the garlic is golden brown, 2 to 3 minutes. Use a slotted spoon to transfer the chickpeas and garlic to a paper towel–lined plate.

3. While the crispy chickpeas are still hot, sprinkle them with half of the lemon zest and with salt and black pepper to taste. Wipe out the pot.

4. Heat the remaining 2 tablespoons oil in the pot over medium-high heat. Add the onion and cook until soft and golden brown, 5 minutes. Stir in the minced garlic, oregano, remaining ¾ teaspoon salt, and the red pepper flakes and cook until fragrant, 1 minute. Add the remaining drained chickpeas, the greens, and stock and bring to a simmer. Reduce the heat to medium-low and cook, covered, until the greens are very tender, 25 to 30 minutes, stirring the pot once or twice.

5. Stir in the feta, the remaining lemon zest, and the juice from half a lemon. Taste and add more salt and lemon juice, if needed. To serve, ladle the stew into individual bowls and top with some of the crispy chickpeas and garlic. Drizzle with oil, sprinkle with parsley and red pepper flakes, if you like, and add another squeeze of lemon.

Orzo Minestrone

with Fresh Corn, Zucchini, and Pesto

SERVES 6 TO 8

¼ cup extra-virgin olive oil, plus more for drizzling

1 medium carrot, cut into ½-inch pieces

1 celery stalk, sliced

1 medium onion, diced

2½ teaspoons kosher salt, divided, plus more as needed

½ teaspoon freshly ground black pepper, plus more for serving

1 medium zucchini, cut into ½-inch pieces

4 garlic cloves, grated or minced

1 (15.5-ounce) can cannellini beans, drained and rinsed

4 cups chicken or vegetable stock

1 (28-ounce) can diced or whole plum tomatoes

1 cup corn kernels, fresh (from 1 large ear) or frozen and thawed

½ cup orzo

1 pint (8 ounces) cherry tomatoes, quartered

¼ cup prepared pesto, plus more for serving

Grated Parmesan cheese, for serving

Torn fresh basil leaves, for serving

My husband, Daniel, calls this "summerstrone," and it's easy to see why. Filled with sweet corn and fresh cherry tomatoes bathed in pesto, it's on the lighter side of minestrone, and perfect for those cool September evenings when there's still loads of fresh corn in the markets but it's not too hot to simmer up a pot of soup. Or use frozen corn to make this in the icy throes of winter. It will be a happy reminder that summer will, eventually, return.

1. In a soup pot, heat the oil over medium-high heat. Stir in the carrot, celery, onion, 1 teaspoon of the salt, and the pepper and cook until softened, stirring frequently, about 5 minutes. Stir in the zucchini and garlic and cook for another 1 minute.

2. Add the beans, stock, canned tomatoes and their liquid, and remaining 1½ teaspoons salt. (If using whole plum tomatoes, break them up with kitchen shears or squish them in your hands before adding them to the pot.) Bring the mixture to a simmer, then cover the pot and reduce the heat to low. Simmer until the vegetables are tender, 20 to 30 minutes. Stir in the corn and orzo, then return to a simmer. Cook until the orzo is nearly tender, 10 to 12 minutes. Taste and add salt, if needed.

3. While the soup is simmering, in a medium bowl, toss together the cherry tomatoes and pesto.

4. When the orzo is almost tender, add the tomatoes and pesto to the pot and simmer for 1 to 2 minutes longer to heat the tomatoes through and finish cooking the orzo. Remove from the heat and ladle the soup into serving bowls. Serve drizzled with a little more oil and topped with more pesto, Parmesan, basil leaves, and lots of pepper.

VEGAN UPGRADE

Skip the Parmesan and make this with prepared vegan pesto, or leave the pesto out entirely and add a couple of grated garlic cloves, a pinch of salt, and ½ cup finely chopped fresh basil to the tomatoes in Step 3.

Shiitake, Sweet Potato, and Tofu Soup

with Miso

SERVES 4 TO 6

1½ tablespoons toasted sesame oil, plus more for drizzling

2 medium sweet potatoes (about 1 pound), peeled and cut into ¾-inch cubes

4 scallions, thinly sliced (white and green parts separated)

4 ounces shiitake mushrooms, stems discarded and caps thinly sliced (about 2 cups)

1-inch piece fresh ginger, peeled and sliced into ¼-inch-thick coins

1 teaspoon kosher salt, plus more to taste

5 cups vegetable stock

1 (4 × 5-inch) piece kombu (optional)

6 tablespoons white or yellow miso, plus more as needed

4 ounces (about 4 cups) baby spinach, torn

1 (12- to 14-ounce) package silken or soft tofu, cut into ¾-inch cubes

Cubes of sweet potato give the miso broth a plush texture and gently sweet flavor in this light soup while the silken tofu adds heft and a good dose of protein. Kombu, a type of dried seaweed, adds umami depth here. To use it, take it out of the package but don't rinse it or wipe it—that white powdery substance on the surface contains natural salts and minerals that contribute to its flavor. If you can't find kombu, stir in a little soy sauce instead. It won't give you the same character but will lend some toasted, salty complexity to the mix.

1. In a large pot over medium heat, heat the oil. Stir in the sweet potatoes, scallion whites and most of the greens (reserve a couple tablespoons for garnish), mushrooms, ginger, and a pinch of salt. Cook until the vegetables are softened but not browning, 5 to 7 minutes.

2. Raise the heat to medium-high and add the stock, 2 cups water, and the 1 teaspoon salt. Place the kombu (if using) on top of everything. Bring to a boil, then reduce the heat and simmer, partially covered, for 10 to 15 minutes, stirring occasionally, until the sweet potatoes are tender.

3. Remove the kombu with tongs or a fork and, once it's cool enough to handle, chop it into pieces and set aside. Ladle about ½ cup soup into a medium bowl and whisk in the miso. Stir the miso mixture back into the pot. Add the spinach, tofu, and reserved chopped kombu, and stir until the spinach wilts. Taste, stirring in more miso and salt, if needed. To serve, ladle into bowls and top with the remaining scallion greens and a drizzle of oil.

SWAP IT OUT

Slivered napa or green cabbage can be substituted for the spinach. Add it along with the sweet potatoes in Step 1 so it has a chance to cook down until very tender.

VEG IT UP

You can double the mushrooms and the spinach to turn this light soup into more of a vegetable-focused stew.

Instant Pots
& Multicookers

Cheater's Chicken and Dumplings

SERVES 4 TO 6

3 pounds bone-in, skin-on chicken pieces, preferably dark meat

1½ teaspoons kosher salt, plus more as needed

½ teaspoon freshly ground black pepper

4 tablespoons (½ stick) unsalted butter, divided

3 celery stalks, diced

2 carrots, diced

1 Spanish onion, diced

4 garlic cloves, smashed and peeled

1 bay leaf

4 cups chicken stock, homemade (page 247) or store-bought

1 pound gnocchi (fresh, frozen, or shelf-stable all work)

4 ounces green beans, trimmed and cut into 1-inch pieces

1 cup chopped fresh parsley or celery leaves

1 teaspoon apple cider vinegar, plus more to taste

Smoked paprika, for serving (optional)

There are two major shortcuts in this cheater's (but still deeply flavorful) take on a Southern classic. The first is that instead of making dumplings from scratch, I use packaged potato gnocchi, which are, after all, technically dumplings, and make for an especially hearty dish. The second is that I don't bother browning *all* the chicken pieces. I only brown as many as fit in the pot for one batch. Since the skin is discarded after cooking, there's no need to stand there getting splattered by chicken fat for any longer than you have to, which is just long enough to build a caramelized layer on the bottom of the pot to add flavor to the broth. This comforting recipe takes some time to put together, but it's still doable on a weeknight, and worth every minute.

1. In a large bowl, toss the chicken pieces with the salt and pepper and set aside while prepping the other ingredients.

2. In the pot of an electric pressure cooker, using the sauté function set on high, melt 2 tablespoons of the butter. Add as many chicken pieces as will fit in a single layer (without crowding) and brown them on all sides until they're a deep golden brown, about 5 minutes per side. Transfer the browned chicken back into the bowl with the remaining unbrowned pieces. You don't need to brown the rest of the chicken.

3. Add the remaining 2 tablespoons butter to the pot and stir in the celery, carrots, onion, garlic, and bay leaf. Sauté until softened, about 12 minutes.

4. Stir in the chicken stock, scraping up any browned bits from the bottom of the pot. Nestle in all the chicken along with the accumulated juices in the bowl. Seal the pot and cook on high pressure for 13 minutes.

(recipe continues)

5. Manually release the pressure and open the pot. Transfer the chicken pieces to a plate and pluck out the bay leaf. When the chicken is cool enough to handle, remove the bones and skin and shred the meat into chunks (you can save the bones and skin to make stock, if you like).

6. Switching back to the sauté function, bring the soup to a boil. Stir in the gnocchi and cook for 5 minutes. Add the green beans and cook for another 5 to 8 minutes, until the beans and gnocchi are tender and the broth thickens. Stir the chicken back into the pot to warm it up. Turn off the pressure cooker and stir in the parsley and vinegar, then taste and add more salt and vinegar, if needed. Serve sprinkled with smoked paprika, if you like.

VEG IT UP

Stir 4 to 5 ounces (4 to 5 cups) baby spinach or kale, or 1 cup thawed frozen peas or corn kernels into the pot with the green beans. Or stir 2 cups diced ripe tomatoes into the pot with the gnocchi.

Spicy Gochujang Chicken Stew

with Potatoes and Cabbage

4 tablespoons soy sauce, divided

2 tablespoons gochujang (or substitute another chile paste, such as Sriracha or sambal oelek)

1 tablespoon honey or brown sugar

2 teaspoons rice vinegar, plus more for serving

⅛ teaspoon gochugaru or other red chile flakes, plus more to taste

2 pounds boneless, skinless chicken thighs

Kosher salt

2 tablespoons neutral oil, such as grapeseed, sunflower, or safflower

1 medium yellow onion, chopped (about 1 cup)

3 medium carrots, sliced into ½-inch rounds (about 1½ cups)

4 garlic cloves, finely grated or minced

2 tablespoons finely grated or minced fresh ginger

1 pound napa cabbage or green cabbage, thinly sliced (about 8 cups)

1 pound potatoes, preferably Yukon Gold, scrubbed and cut into 1½-inch cubes

4 scallions, thinly sliced

½ cup fresh cilantro leaves and tender stems, coarsely chopped

Loosely based on a traditional Korean chicken stew called dak dori tang or dakjjim, this spicy, homey dish is the very essence of full-flavored comfort food—chock-full of potatoes, carrots, and green cabbage that softens into silky strands as it simmers. If you can't get the gochujang (a glossy, mildly sweet Korean chile paste) or gochugaru (spicy Korean chile flakes), I've given substitutes. But I encourage you to seek them out, especially if you love spicy, complex flavors. Then use them anywhere you want to add a little oomph—they're great in sauces and glazes, added to egg dishes, or stirred into marinades for tofu, meat, or fish.

1. In a large bowl, whisk together 3 tablespoons of the soy sauce, the gochujang, honey, vinegar, and gochugaru. Season the chicken thighs all over with salt and add them to the bowl; let them marinate at room temperature while you brown the onion and carrots.

2. In the pot of an electric pressure cooker, using the sauté function, heat the oil until hot, about 20 seconds. Add the onion, carrots, and a pinch of salt to the pot and cook, stirring occasionally, until the vegetables begin to brown and soften slightly, about 7 minutes.

3. Stir in the garlic and ginger and cook until fragrant, 1 minute. Stir in ½ cup water and bring to a simmer, scraping up the browned bits on the bottom of the pot so they won't burn.

4. Stir in the cabbage and sprinkle with a generous pinch or two of salt. Add the potatoes and the chicken along with all its marinade.

5. Seal the pot and cook on high pressure for 10 minutes. Manually release the pressure.

6. Stir in the remaining 1 tablespoon soy sauce. Taste and season with more salt and vinegar, if needed. Garnish with the sliced scallions and cilantro and serve.

(see following page for tips)

OUR SIGNATURE
GO-CHU-JANG

The unique fermentation
process (think miso meets
chile) creates an unparall-
eled spicy umami flavor.
Add this "secret ingredient"
to your cooking for a
lingering finish that makes
everything delicious.

Discoloration and overflow
may occur due to the raw,
active fermentation.
Separation is natural, mix
before use.

BEST BY : 28FEB2023

MADE WITH NON-GMO INGREDIENTS.
PRODUCT OF SOUTH KOREA.
PACKED IN THE USA.
REFRIGERATE AFTER OPENING.

Nutrition Facts Servings: 13, Serv. Size: 1 Tbsp (22g), Calories 45

SWAP IT OUT

To substitute chicken
breasts for the thighs, cut the
potatoes into 1-inch cubes
and cook the stew on high
pressure for 8 minutes.

VEG IT UP

Stir 4 to 5 ounces (4 to
5 cups) baby spinach or baby
kale into the pot along with
the soy sauce in Step 6.

VEG IT UP

This is a perfect dish for adding greens. Stir in 4 to 5 ounces (4 to 5 cups) of chopped baby spinach, kale, or chard before adding the sour cream. Let the greens wilt (turning on the sauté function for 1 or 2 minutes, if needed), then stir in the sour cream and dill.

Chicken Paprikash Soup

with Potatoes and Quick Pickled Cucumbers

SERVES 4

FOR THE CHICKEN

2 tablespoons extra-virgin olive oil

2 tablespoons unsalted butter

2 large onions, diced

4 garlic cloves, minced

2 tablespoons sweet paprika, plus more for serving

1 teaspoon hot paprika (or smoked paprika if you like it smoky)

⅔ cup chicken stock, homemade (page 247) or store-bought

1½ pounds Yukon Gold or baby potatoes, cut into 1-inch chunks

2¾ teaspoons kosher salt, divided, plus more as needed

Freshly ground black pepper

2¼ to 2½ pounds boneless, skinless chicken thighs

⅔ cup sour cream (or you can use whole-milk Greek yogurt)

⅓ cup fresh dill, chopped, plus more for serving

FOR THE QUICK PICKLED CUCUMBERS

⅓ cup apple cider vinegar

1 teaspoon sugar

½ teaspoon kosher salt

2 Persian cucumbers, very thinly sliced

Seasoned with two kinds of paprika, dill, loads of garlic, and sour cream, this thick and homey chicken soup (almost a stew) was loosely inspired by paprikash and my Budapest dreams. The quality of your paprika makes a big difference here, so if you can't remember when you last bought a fresh jar, now would be a very good time. The pickled cucumbers balance the creamy broth, cutting its richness with a jolt of cider vinegar. But you can skip it if it's just one step too many. Also, if you'd rather eat this with noodles instead of potatoes (more traditional, but not a one-pot meal), simply leave out the potatoes and boil up some noodles while the chicken braises in the pressure cooker.

1. Prepare the chicken: In the pot of an electric pressure cooker, using the sauté function set on high if possible, heat the oil and butter. Stir in the onions and cook until translucent, 4 to 6 minutes. Reduce the sauté function to medium if you can, then stir in the garlic and cook for 30 seconds. Stir in the sweet and hot paprikas and cook for another 30 seconds.

2. Stir in the stock, potatoes, and ¾ teaspoon of the salt. Season the chicken with the remaining 2 teaspoons salt and lots of pepper, then nestle it on top of the broth and onions.

3. Seal the pot and cook on high pressure for 8 minutes. Let the pressure release naturally for 10 minutes, then manually release the remaining pressure.

4. Meanwhile, **prepare the quick pickled cucumbers:** In a medium bowl, stir together the vinegar, sugar, and salt until dissolved. Stir in the cucumbers and let them sit, tossing occasionally, until ready to serve (at least 10 minutes or up to a few days; store them in the fridge if keeping longer than 4 hours).

5. When the pressure is released, open the lid and stir in the sour cream and dill. Taste and add more salt, if necessary.

6. Serve the soup in bowls topped with more dill and a sprinkle of sweet paprika, with the cucumbers either on the side or nestled into the bowl.

1 pound **beef stew meat**, cut into ½-inch cubes

2 teaspoons **kosher salt**, divided, plus more as needed

½ teaspoon **freshly ground black pepper**, plus more as needed

2 tablespoons **extra-virgin olive oil**, plus more as needed

3 small or 2 large **leeks**, white and light green parts, halved lengthwise and thinly sliced into half moons

3 **celery stalks**, diced (save the leaves for garnish)

1 **fennel bulb**, diced

4 **garlic cloves**, finely chopped

1 tablespoon **tomato paste**

¾ teaspoon **ground coriander**

½ teaspoon **ground cumin**

½ teaspoon **paprika**

4 cups **beef, chicken, or vegetable stock**

3 fresh **sage** sprigs

2 fresh **rosemary** sprigs

2 **bay leaves**

2 **carrots**, cut into ½-inch chunks

¾ cup **pearled barley**

8 ounces (8 cups) **baby spinach or baby kale**

¼ cup chopped fresh **parsley**

Finely grated zest of 1 large **lemon**, plus fresh **lemon juice** to taste

Thinly sliced **jalapeños** or other **chiles**, seeded if desired, for serving (optional)

Lemony Beef, Spinach, and Barley Soup

Filled with baby spinach and seasoned with lively lemon and heady spices, this beef barley soup is lighter and brighter than many of its kind. But it still makes for a substantial, stick-to-your-ribs kind of meal. If you like a kick, don't neglect the jalapeño at the end. It will wilt slightly from the heat of the soup, adding zip and freshness to the mix. This makes a lot of soup, but leftovers freeze well for up to 6 months.

1. Season the beef with 1 teaspoon of the salt and the pepper. Let it stand at room temperature for 30 minutes to 1 hour.

2. In the pot of an electric pressure cooker set to sauté, heat the oil. Add the beef and cook in batches, turning occasionally, until lightly browned, 5 to 7 minutes per batch. Drizzle in more oil if the pot seems dry. Transfer the beef to a plate as it browns.

3. Add the leeks, celery, fennel, and garlic to the pot; cook until soft, about 8 minutes. Push the vegetables to one side and if the pot looks dry, add a bit more oil. Add the tomato paste, coriander, cumin, and paprika to the cleared spot and cook until the tomato paste is darkened and caramelized, about 1 minute. Stir the vegetables and tomato paste together.

4. Return the beef to the pot. Add ½ cup water and let it come to a simmer, scraping up the bottom of the pot to remove the brown bits. Add the stock. Using kitchen string, tie the sage, rosemary, and bay leaves into a bundle and drop into the pot (or just drop them in the pot untied and fish them out after cooking). Stir in the carrots, barley, and the remaining 1 teaspoon salt.

5. Seal the pot and cook on high pressure for 25 minutes. Let the pressure release naturally for 10 minutes, then manually release the remaining pressure. Uncover the pot and pull the herb bunch from the pot and discard.

6. Stir the spinach and parsley into the pot until wilted, 2 to 3 minutes (kale might take a few minutes longer), then stir in the lemon zest and juice. If the soup is too thick, thin it down with a little water. Taste and add more salt, pepper, and lemon juice, if necessary. Serve with chiles, if you like.

VEG IT UP

You can double the amount of spinach here.

SLOW IT DOWN

To make this in a slow cooker, brown the pork and sauté the vegetables in a skillet for Steps 3 and 4. Then, after adding the tomatoes, pour everything into the slow cooker along with the pork. Cook on low for 7 to 8 hours or on high for 5 to 6 hours.

Pork Stew

with Sweet Peppers and Potatoes

SERVES 4 TO 6

2 pounds boneless pork butt (fat trimmed) or pork stew meat, cut into 1½-inch pieces

3 tablespoons fresh oregano, finely chopped

2½ teaspoons kosher salt, divided, plus more as needed

½ teaspoon freshly ground black pepper, divided

¼ teaspoon crushed red pepper flakes

1 teaspoon fennel seeds

3 tablespoons extra-virgin olive oil, divided

3 red, yellow, or orange bell peppers, sliced ½ inch thick

1 large onion, thinly sliced

4 garlic cloves, finely grated or minced

1 cup diced tomatoes (canned or fresh)

1½ pounds Yukon Gold potatoes, cut into 1-inch chunks (either peeled or unpeeled)

5 ounces (5 cups) baby spinach, coarsely chopped

½ cup chopped fresh parsley leaves and tender stems, plus more for serving

Lemon wedges, for serving (optional)

Seasoned with sweet peppers, fresh oregano, and fennel seeds, and filled with creamy Yukon Gold potatoes, this pork stew has tender chunks of meat surrounded by a richly flavored broth that's so good, you'll want to slurp it from a spoon. To save time, I only brown one batch of the pork—just what fits comfortably in a single layer in the pot. This is enough to create a fond (those caramelized brown bits on the bottom of the pot) that adds intensity to the sauce. Like all stews, this one is even better the next day, and will keep for at least 5 days in the fridge. But don't freeze the leftovers; the potatoes tend to get mushy after defrosting.

1. In a large bowl, toss the pork with the oregano, 1½ teaspoons of the salt, ¼ teaspoon of the black pepper, and the red pepper flakes and set aside while chopping and preparing the other ingredients.

2. Using a mortar and pestle or the flat side of a chef's knife and a cutting board, crack the fennel seeds lightly.

3. In the pot of an electric pressure cooker, using the sauté function set on high, heat 2 tablespoons of the oil. Add as many pork pieces as will fit in a single layer (without crowding), and brown on all sides until deep golden brown, about 4 minutes per side. Transfer the browned pork back into the bowl with the remaining unbrowned pieces. You don't need to brown the rest of the pork.

4. Add the remaining 1 tablespoon oil and stir in the peppers and onion. Sauté until softened, about 8 minutes. Add the garlic, cracked fennel seeds, the remaining 1 teaspoon salt, and the remaining ¼ teaspoon black pepper, and cook for 1 minute, until fragrant. Stir in the tomatoes, scraping up any browned bits from the bottom of the pot. Add the potatoes and the pork along with the accumulated juices in the bowl.

5. Seal the pot and cook on high pressure for 22 minutes. Let the pressure release naturally for 10 minutes, then release the remaining pressure.

6. Remove the lid and stir in the spinach and parsley, stirring until the greens wilt. Taste and add more salt, if needed. Serve sprinkled with more parsley and a squeeze of lemon, if using.

Smoky Lentil Stew

with Kielbasa and Potatoes

SERVES 4 TO 6

2 tablespoons extra-virgin olive oil, plus more for drizzling

2 leeks, white and light green parts, halved lengthwise and thinly sliced into half moons

8 ounces smoked kielbasa (or whatever sausage you like), cut into ¾-inch cubes

3 garlic cloves, finely grated or minced

1½ teaspoons smoked paprika, plus more for serving

Pinch of ground cayenne

1 (14.5-ounce) can diced tomatoes

1 bay leaf

1 large fresh rosemary sprig

1 teaspoon kosher salt, plus more as needed

Freshly ground black pepper

1½ cups dried green or brown lentils

1½ pounds potatoes, peeled and cut into ¾-inch cubes

1 teaspoon sherry vinegar (or use cider or white wine vinegar), plus more to taste

½ cup chopped fresh parsley or cilantro leaves and tender stems, plus more for serving

Quick-cooking lentils are a boon to legume-loving cooks in a hurry. Here, they're simmered into a thick, nubby stew filled with soft chunks of potato and smoky pieces of kielbasa. Don't neglect the herbs and vinegar at the end, as their brightness and tang make a huge difference and keep this from falling into stodgy territory.

1. In the pot of an electric pressure cooker, using the sauté function, heat the oil until hot. Add the leeks and kielbasa and sauté until lightly browned, 8 to 10 minutes. Stir in the garlic, paprika, and cayenne, and cook for another minute, until the garlic is fragrant.

2. Stir in the tomatoes, bay leaf, rosemary, salt, and a generous pinch or two of black pepper, scraping up any browned bits from the bottom of the pot. Stir in the lentils, potatoes, and 1½ cups water.

3. Seal the pot and cook on high pressure for 11 minutes. Allow the pressure to release naturally.

4. Discard the bay leaf and rosemary. Stir the vinegar and parsley into the lentils; taste and add more vinegar and/or salt, if needed. If the stew is too thick, add a few splashes of water to thin it down. To serve, ladle the stew into bowls and sprinkle with more parsley and paprika, and drizzle with oil.

VEG IT UP

Add 2 sliced carrots or celery stalks (or 1 of each), or 1 cup of diced turnips, to the pot along with the tomatoes. Add 4 to 5 ounces (4 to 5 cups) chopped baby spinach or kale, or 1 pint of halved cherry tomatoes once the stew is finished. After discarding the bay leaf and rosemary in Step 4, add the veggies to the hot lentils, stirring, until they are just softened, 2 minutes.

VEGAN UPGRADE

Nix the sausage and increase the smoked paprika slightly (do it to taste at the end). Or substitute some vegan sausage, if you like, but this hearty, flavorful stew doesn't really need it.

Red Wine, Mushroom, and Pancetta Risotto

SERVES 4

3 tablespoons extra-virgin olive oil

4 ounces pancetta, diced

8 ounces mushrooms, sliced

1 leek, white and light green parts, halved and thinly sliced (or use 2 shallots)

2 garlic cloves, minced

3 to 3½ cups chicken or vegetable stock

1½ cups Arborio rice

1½ teaspoons kosher salt, plus more to taste

1 cup fruity red wine (Côtes du Rhône or Cabernet, for example)

Freshly ground black pepper

Chopped fresh parsley or dill, for serving

Freshly grated Parmesan cheese, for serving (optional)

VEGAN UPGRADE

Skip the Parmesan and pancetta and add an extra 4 ounces of mushrooms to the pot. If you like, you can finish this with a sprinkling of nutritional yeast, though there's enough going on that you wouldn't miss it.

Most risotto recipes call for white wine, in part to maintain the pure pale color of the rice. But using red wine adds richness and a more pronounced fruitiness to the pot. Beware the color though. Depending on what kind of red wine you use, the risotto may end up anywhere from burgundy to puce to kind of gray. Luckily, a handful of parsley will cure all, and the depth of flavor makes up for the hue. You can use any kind of mushroom, but maitakes are my favorite here for their lacy texture and intensely woodsy flavor.

1. In the pot of an electric pressure cooker, using the sauté function set on medium, heat 1 tablespoon of the oil until hot. Add the pancetta and cook, stirring occasionally, until golden and crisp on all sides, 6 to 8 minutes. Transfer the pancetta to a paper towel–lined plate.

2. Raise the sauté heat to high and stir in the mushrooms and leek. Cook, stirring occasionally, until just browned, 7 to 9 minutes. Stir in the garlic and cook for 1 minute longer, until fragrant.

3. Use a slotted spoon to transfer the mushroom mixture to a 4-cup measuring cup, then pour enough stock into the measuring cup so that the mushrooms and liquid together make 3½ cups.

4. Reduce the heat to medium and add the remaining 2 tablespoons oil to the pot. Stir in the rice and salt, and cook until lightly toasted, stirring occasionally, about 3 minutes. Stir in the wine and a generous amount of pepper and cook until all the liquid is absorbed by the rice, 1 to 2 minutes. Stir in the mushroom-stock mixture and half of the cooked pancetta.

5. Seal the pot and cook on high pressure for 6 minutes. Manually release the pressure, then stir until the risotto is nice and creamy, about 2 minutes. Taste and add more salt and pepper, if necessary. Serve sprinkled with the remaining crispy pancetta, parsley, and Parmesan, if desired.

Spicy Tomato
White Beans

with Sage, Pecorino, and Garlicky Crostini

SERVES 4 TO 6

1 pound dried white beans, such as cannellini or Great Northern beans

2 teaspoons kosher salt, plus more as needed

2 tablespoons extra-virgin olive oil, plus more for drizzling

6 garlic cloves: 4 thinly sliced, 2 halved

1 large red onion, thinly sliced

1 (28-ounce) can crushed tomatoes

1 tablespoon chopped fresh sage leaves (or use rosemary)

1 bay leaf

¼ teaspoon crushed red pepper flakes, plus more for serving

Freshly ground black pepper

4 to 6 large slices crusty bread

Grated pecorino Romano cheese, for garnish

½ cup torn fresh parsley leaves and tender stems, for garnish

Fresh ricotta, for serving (optional)

Oil-packed anchovy fillets, for serving (optional)

The only thing that I like better than a simple, homey bowl of tomatoey white beans spiked with chile flakes and eaten with garlicky crostini is when I have the forethought to garnish it all with a dollop of creamy ricotta and an anchovy draped over the toast. When I can plan ahead, I like to soak the beans in advance. They cook up more evenly. But don't let unsoaked beans stop you from making this fragrant, soul-satisfying dish. I've given instructions for using both soaked and unsoaked beans.

1. If you are thinking ahead, soak the white beans: Put them in a bowl with enough water to cover them by 4 inches and stir in 1 tablespoon of salt. Let soak for 4 to 24 hours. Drain and rinse. If you didn't soak the beans, just give them a rinse.

2. In the pot of an electric pressure cooker, using the sauté function, heat the oil until hot. Stir in the sliced garlic, onion, and a pinch of salt and cook until golden brown, 3 to 4 minutes. Stir in the beans, tomatoes, sage, bay leaf, the 2 teaspoons salt, red pepper flakes, and a lot of black pepper.

3. If you've soaked the beans, add enough water to just cover them. If you have not soaked them, you'll need to add more water, enough to cover them by a good inch. Seal the pot and cook on high pressure for 13 minutes for soaked beans and 26 minutes for unsoaked beans.

4. Allow the pressure to release naturally for 10 minutes, then release the remaining pressure. Taste a bean or two—if they aren't done, cook on high pressure for another 2 to 4 minutes, depending on how hard they seem to you. Manually release the pressure; remove the bay leaf. Taste and add more salt and black pepper, if needed.

5. Just before serving, toast the bread and rub both sides of each piece with the cut side of the halved garlic cloves. I find it easiest to start by rubbing the crusts, which helps break down the cloves and releases the oil. Then drizzle each piece of garlicky toast with oil and season lightly with salt.

6. To serve, sprinkle the beans with pecorino, red pepper flakes, and black pepper. Drizzle with oil, top with the parsley, and eat with the toast, dunking it into the savory sauce. If you're using the ricotta, plop some into the bowl. And if you're using anchovies, drape one or two over each crostini. Yum.

VEG IT UP

There are so many ways to add veggies to this stew. You can stir in 1 to 2 cups diced carrots or celery with the beans in Step 2. You can sauté 4 ounces diced mushrooms with the onions in Step 2 (just add a few minutes onto the sautéing time so they turn golden brown). You can mix in baby greens—add 4 to 5 ounces (4 to 5 cups) chopped spinach, kale, chard, or pea shoots in Step 4—and stir until they wilt (turn the sauté function on if they seem to need a little more heat). Fresh diced tomatoes are lovely added at the end for garnish. Spoon some into each bowl before you sprinkle on the pecorino.

VEGAN UPGRADE

Skip the pecorino and, if you like, garnish each bowl with a sprinkling of nutritional yeast for extra umami.

SLOW IT DOWN

Sauté the onion and garlic in Step 2 in a skillet, then scrape it into a slow cooker and add the remaining ingredients as called for, plus an extra few cups of water. Cook on high for 2½ to 4 hours, or on low for 4 to 7 hours (the longer cooking range here depends on whether you've soaked your beans).

Farro and Kale Stew

with Parmesan and Creamy Burrata

SERVES 4 TO 6

2 tablespoons extra-virgin olive oil, plus more for serving

2 fat garlic cloves, thinly sliced

2 shallots or 1 small onion, thinly sliced

12 ounces curly or lacinato kale, stems removed, leaves coarsely chopped (10 cups)

½ teaspoon kosher salt, plus more as needed

Freshly ground black pepper

3 cups vegetable or chicken stock

Parmesan rind (optional)

1 teaspoon fresh thyme leaves

Pinch of crushed red pepper flakes, plus more for serving

1¼ cups pearled or semi-pearled farro

¼ cup grated Parmesan cheese, plus more to taste

6 to 8 ounces burrata, for serving

Flaky sea salt, for serving

In this thick and multitextured stew, chewy farro and silky kale are cooked in a Parmesan-enriched broth, then topped with creamy burrata. The cheese adds plenty of richness while healthful whole grains and greens keep it firmly anchored in good-for-you territory. If you have a Parmesan rind on hand, feel free to toss it into the pot with the stock.

1. In the pot of an electric pressure cooker, using the sauté function, combine the oil, garlic, and shallots. Cook, stirring, until the garlic and shallots are golden brown, 2 to 4 minutes. Stir in the kale, a pinch of kosher salt, and plenty of black pepper and cook until the greens are slightly wilted, about 2 minutes.

2. Stir in the stock, Parmesan rind (if using), thyme, ½ teaspoon kosher salt, and the red pepper flakes, scraping up any browned bits from the bottom of the pot. Stir in the farro.

3. Seal the pot and cook on high pressure for 7 minutes. Allow the pressure to release naturally for 5 minutes, then release the remaining pressure manually.

4. Open the pot and stir in the grated Parmesan; taste and add more Parmesan and kosher salt, if needed. To serve, ladle the stew into bowls and top with pieces of burrata. Sprinkle with flaky sea salt, oil, and more red pepper flakes, if you like.

SWAP IT OUT

You can use any sturdy greens here in place of the kale. Mustard greens, collards, or even broccoli rabe will all work well in the pot.

SLOW IT DOWN

Use a skillet to sauté the vegetables in Step 1, then transfer them to a slow cooker along with the remaining ingredients from Step 2 and cook on low for 4 to 5 hours or on high for 2 to 3 hours, adding more liquid if the mixture dries out at any point.

Curried Sweet Potato and Lentil Soup

with Crispy Coconut Chips

SERVES 4 TO 6

⅓ cup unsweetened coconut flakes, for serving

3 tablespoons coconut oil

1 pound sweet potatoes, peeled and cut into ¾-inch cubes (about 3 cups)

1 yellow onion, chopped

3 fat garlic cloves, minced

1 tablespoon grated fresh ginger

1 jalapeño, seeded if you like, diced

2 teaspoons kosher salt, plus more to taste

1 tablespoon garam masala

½ teaspoon ground turmeric

3 cups vegetable stock

1 (13.5-ounce) can unsweetened full-fat coconut milk

1 cup red lentils, rinsed

5 ounces (about 5 cups) baby spinach, coarsely chopped

1 tablespoon freshly squeezed lime juice

½ cup chopped fresh cilantro leaves and tender stems, for serving

Flaky sea salt, for serving

This boldly spiced soup is wonderfully thick and creamy from the combination of coconut milk and puréed sweet potatoes. The red lentils break down completely in the pressure cooker, adding protein and heft but without their usual nubby texture, so there's nothing to interrupt the velvety character of the broth. A garnish of toasted coconut flakes provides some crunch at the end. But if you don't want to bother toasting, better to leave the coconut flakes out altogether; untoasted chips just aren't that pleasant to eat with this soup.

1. In the pot of an electric pressure cooker, using the sauté function, toast the coconut flakes, stirring often, until they are fragrant and pale golden at the edges, 1 to 3 minutes. Transfer to a plate to cool.

2. Add the oil to the pot and let it heat for a few seconds. Stir in the sweet potatoes and onion and cook until golden brown, 8 to 10 minutes. Add the garlic, ginger, jalapeño, salt, garam masala, and turmeric and cook until fragrant, 1 to 2 minutes. Stir in the stock, coconut milk, and lentils.

3. Seal the pot and cook on high pressure for 6 minutes. Allow the pressure to release naturally for 10 minutes, then release the remaining pressure manually (or you can just let the pressure release naturally if you're not in a hurry).

4. Open the pot and stir in the spinach until just wilted, about 2 minutes. (If the soup has cooled down, you might have to turn the sauté function on to heat it back up.) Stir in the lime juice and season with kosher salt to taste. To serve, ladle the soup into bowls and sprinkle with cilantro, toasted coconut flakes, and flaky sea salt to taste.

VEG IT UP

Add 2 diced carrots or 3 diced turnips to the pot along with the sweet potatoes.

One-Bowl Cakes

Blueberry Lime Crunch Cake with Demerara

SERVES 8

12 tablespoons (1½ sticks / 170 grams) unsalted butter, melted and cooled, plus more for the pan

1½ cups (337 grams) sour cream, at room temperature

4 large eggs, at room temperature

1 teaspoon fine sea salt

1¼ cups (250 grams) granulated sugar

1 tablespoon finely grated lime zest (from 2 limes)

1½ teaspoons baking powder

½ teaspoon baking soda

1 teaspoon ground cinnamon

2½ cups (312 grams) all-purpose flour

1½ cups (200 grams) fresh blueberries (or frozen, unthawed)

⅔ cup (57 grams) sliced almonds (or chopped walnuts or pecans)

2 tablespoons Demerara sugar

This might just be the easiest and crunchiest coffee cake you've ever made. It's also one of the best—filled with soft, juicy blueberries that are flavored with tart bursts of lime zest and nestled into a cinnamon-scented batter. Instead of a classic crumb topping, the surface is strewn with Demerara sugar and sliced almonds, which bake into a gorgeously crisp contrast to the velvety crumb below. It will keep at room temperature for up to 3 days, though the topping does lose a little texture the longer it sits. But with a cake this good, its keeping qualities may be beside the point.

1. Heat the oven to 350°F and butter a 9 × 9-inch metal pan. If you like, you can line the pan with parchment paper, leaving an overhang on two sides so you can lift the cake out after it cools. But if you plan to serve the cake directly from the pan, you don't need to do this.

2. In a large bowl, whisk together the sour cream, butter, eggs, and salt until everything is well combined. Whisk in the granulated sugar and lime zest. Whisk in the dry ingredients in this order: baking powder, baking soda, and cinnamon. Then whisk in the flour until just combined. Fold in the blueberries.

3. Scrape the batter into the prepared pan, smoothing the top. Sprinkle with the almonds and Demerara sugar. Bake until the top is golden and puffed, and a toothpick inserted into the center of the cake comes out clean, 50 to 60 minutes. Transfer the cake to a wire rack and let it cool still in the pan.

SWAP IT OUT

You can substitute full-fat Greek yogurt for the sour cream. And other spices, like cardamom, ginger, or pumpkin pie spice, can replace the cinnamon. Or leave out the spice for a more subtle cake.

ONE-BOWL CAKES

Cardamom Sour Cream Pound Cake

SERVES 8

8 tablespoons (1 stick / 113 grams) unsalted butter, melted and cooled, plus more for the pan

1 cup (227 grams) sour cream

3 large eggs, at room temperature

1 tablespoon brandy or vanilla extract

¾ teaspoon kosher salt

1¼ cups (250 grams) sugar

1 teaspoon ground cardamom

1¼ teaspoons baking powder

¼ teaspoon baking soda

1⅔ cups (208 grams) all-purpose flour

With a dense and velvety crumb and a deep, musky perfume from the cardamom, this buttery loaf has everything you want in a pound cake. I like to serve thin slices all by themselves with my afternoon tea. Or you can dress it up for a festive dessert, adding tangy crème fraîche and sliced fruit, or a crowd-pleasing scoop of ice cream drizzled with chocolate or caramel sauce, or big yellow dollops of lemon curd. A great pound cake goes with almost everything.

1. Heat the oven to 350°F. Lightly butter an 8 × 4-inch or 9 × 5-inch loaf pan and line it with parchment paper, leaving about 2 inches of excess on each side to help you lift the cake out of the pan.

2. In a large bowl, whisk together the sour cream, butter, eggs, brandy, and salt until everything is well combined. Whisk in the sugar. Whisk in the dry ingredients in this order: cardamom, baking powder, and baking soda, whisking well in between additions. Then whisk in the flour until just combined.

3. Scrape the batter into the prepared loaf pan, smoothing the top. Bake until the top is golden and a toothpick inserted into the center of the cake comes out clean, 45 to 55 minutes. Transfer the cake to a wire rack and let it cool in the pan. To unmold, run a thin spatula or butter knife around the inner edges of the pan, then use the parchment paper to lift the cake onto a platter and slice to serve.

SWAP IT OUT

You can use Greek yogurt in place of the sour cream. And other spices, like cinnamon, ginger, or pumpkin pie spice, can replace the cardamom. Or leave out the spice for a more subtle cake.

Brown Butter Cornmeal Yogurt Cake

SERVES 8

8 tablespoons (1 stick / 113 grams) unsalted butter, plus more for the pan

1 cup (200 grams) sugar

½ cup (123 grams) plain whole-milk yogurt, at room temperature

2 teaspoons vanilla extract (or ¼ teaspoon almond extract)

2 large eggs, at room temperature

1 teaspoon baking powder

¼ teaspoon baking soda

¼ teaspoon kosher salt

¼ teaspoon freshly grated nutmeg (or 1 teaspoon finely grated citrus zest)

1¼ cups (160 grams) all-purpose flour

½ cup (60 grams) fine or medium cornmeal (don't use coarse or the texture will be too crumbly)

Melted butter in a loaf cake is all well and good, but browned butter is even better. Here it lends its deeply nutty, caramelized character to a moist cornmeal yogurt cake that's easy to throw together and then hard to stop eating once you do. Serve slices toasted and buttered for breakfast, plain with tea or coffee for an afternoon snack, or topped with berries and whipped cream for a dreamy dessert.

1. Heat the oven to 350°F. Lightly butter an 8 × 4-inch or 9 × 5-inch loaf pan and line it with parchment paper, leaving about 2 inches of excess on each side to help you lift the cake out of the pan.

2. In a large pot, melt the butter over medium heat. Once it has melted, let it continue to cook until the white foam subsides and the milk solids fall to the bottom of the pot and turn speckly golden brown, the color of hazelnut skins. You'll hear the butter bubble vigorously, then it will quiet down as the moisture evaporates and the butter browns. It can take anywhere from 3 to 7 minutes. Keep an eye on it so it doesn't burn. Remove the pan from the heat and let it cool completely.

3. Whisk the sugar, yogurt, and vanilla into the butter, followed by the eggs, one at a time. Whisk in the dry ingredients in this order: baking powder, baking soda, salt, and nutmeg, whisking well in between additions. Then whisk in the flour and cornmeal until just combined.

4. Scrape the batter into the prepared loaf pan, smoothing the top. Bake until the top is golden and a toothpick inserted into the center of the cake comes out clean, 45 to 55 minutes. Transfer the cake to a wire rack and let it cool in the pan. To unmold, run a thin spatula or butter knife around the inner edges of the pan, then use the parchment paper to lift out the cake.

SWAP IT OUT

You can substitute sour cream or buttermilk for the yogurt.

ADD IT IN

You can add 1 cup of blueberries (fresh, or frozen and unthawed) to the batter.

Ricotta Olive Oil Pound Cake

SERVES 8

Unsalted butter, shortening, or nonstick cooking spray, for the pan

1½ cups (300 grams) sugar, plus more for the pan if using a Bundt pan

3 large eggs, at room temperature

1 cup (250 grams) whole-milk ricotta cheese, at room temperature

½ cup (123 grams) sour cream or plain whole-milk yogurt, at room temperature

¾ cup (97 grams) extra-virgin olive oil

1 tablespoon vanilla extract

2½ teaspoons (10 grams) baking powder

1 teaspoon (5 grams) fine sea salt

1 teaspoon finely grated orange or lemon zest

1½ cups (192 grams) all-purpose flour

This gorgeous golden-topped loaf has a moist and dense crumb that's deeply imbued with orange zest and olive oil. You don't need to break out your very best extra-virgin stuff here, but you should use a good oil that has some character, otherwise the cake won't have the same complex flavor. Or try it with melted butter for something more mellow (see Swap It Out).

1. Heat the oven to 350°F. Lightly grease a 9 × 5-inch loaf pan or a 10 to 12-cup Bundt pan (or spray with nonstick cooking spray). If using a loaf pan, line it with parchment paper, leaving about 2 inches of excess on each side to help you lift the cake out of the pan. If using a Bundt, sprinkle the inside of the pan with sugar, including the center cone.

2. In a large bowl, whisk together the eggs, ricotta, and sour cream until combined. Add the oil and vanilla and mix until well blended. Whisk in the sugar, baking powder, salt, and zest until well combined. Using a rubber spatula, fold in the flour until just incorporated.

3. Scrape the batter into the prepared pan and smooth the top with the spatula. Bake until the cake is golden brown and a toothpick inserted into the center comes out clean, 50 to 65 minutes for the loaf pan, 40 to 55 minutes for the Bundt, rotating the pan halfway through baking.

4. Transfer to a wire rack and let the cake cool in the pan for at least 1 hour before unmolding and slicing.

SWAP IT OUT

To take this in a gentler direction, substitute melted butter for the oil.

Tender Chocolate Coconut Cake

SERVES 8 TO 10

FOR THE CAKE

8 tablespoons (1 stick / 113 grams) unsalted butter, melted and cooled (or ½ cup neutral oil, such as grapeseed, sunflower, or safflower), plus more for the pan

1 large egg, at room temperature

1 cup unsweetened full-fat coconut milk

1 teaspoon vanilla extract

1 teaspoon apple cider vinegar or white vinegar

1 cup (200 grams) granulated sugar

⅓ cup (30 grams) unsweetened cocoa powder

¾ teaspoon baking soda

½ teaspoon fine sea salt

1¼ cups (160 grams) all-purpose flour

¼ cup semisweet chocolate chips (optional)

¼ cup sweetened or unsweetened shredded coconut

FOR THE GLAZE

1 cup confectioners' sugar

¼ cup unsweetened full-fat coconut milk

¼ cup sweetened or unsweetened shredded coconut

With a soft, velvety crumb and shaggy coconut icing, this is on the lighter side of the chocolate cake spectrum, more airy than dense. The glaze, which is poured onto the cake while it's still warm, soaks into the crumb, making it very moist. You can use either sweetened or unsweetened coconut for the glaze. The sweetened kind gives you a candy-like topping that's a little like the filling of a Mounds bar; unsweetened flakes take the sugar quotient down a notch. In either case, it's a pretty, festive cake that comes together in a flash.

1. **Make the cake:** Heat the oven to 350°F. Lightly grease a 9-inch round cake pan or a 9 × 9-inch baking pan and line the bottom with parchment paper (if you're using a square pan, you can leave about 2 inches of excess paper on each side to help you lift the cake out of the pan).

2. In a large bowl, whisk together the butter, egg, coconut milk, vanilla, and vinegar until well combined and smooth. Whisk in the sugar, cocoa powder, baking soda, and salt until smooth, then whisk in the flour last of all.

3. Using a rubber spatula, fold in the chocolate chips, if using, and the shredded coconut until just incorporated.

4. Scrape the batter into the prepared pan and smooth the top with the spatula. Bake until the edges of the cake spring back when lightly pressed and a toothpick inserted into the center comes out clean, 30 to 40 minutes, rotating the pan halfway through baking.

5. Right before the cake comes out of the oven, **make the glaze** (don't do it ahead of time or it will get gloppy): Place the confectioners' sugar in a mixing bowl and whisk in the coconut milk until well combined. When the cake comes out of the oven, use a fork or toothpick to poke holes all over the top of it. Pour the coconut glaze evenly over the warm cake, allowing the glaze to soak into the cake. Sprinkle the shredded coconut on top.

6. Transfer the pan to a wire rack to let the glaze set and the cake cool completely before cutting.

VEGAN UPGRADE

Use oil instead of butter. A flax egg works perfectly here: In a small bowl, mix together 1 tablespoon flaxseed meal with 2½ tablespoons water and let it sit for 5 minutes. Then use in place of the egg.

Easy Chocolate Fudge Torte

SERVES 8 TO 10

12 tablespoons (1½ sticks / 170 grams) **unsalted butter,** melted and cooled, plus more for the pan

1¼ cups (250 grams) **sugar**

½ cup (55 grams) **unsweetened cocoa powder,** preferably Dutch-process, plus more for serving

½ teaspoon **fine sea salt**

4 large **eggs,** at room temperature

1 tablespoon **bourbon or vanilla extract**

¾ cup (92 grams) **all-purpose flour**

Whipped cream or whipped crème fraîche, for serving

Ground cinnamon or cardamom, for serving (optional)

SWAP IT OUT

For a richer, more fudge-like flavor with a hint of bitterness, substitute dark brown sugar for the granulated sugar. To make a gluten-free flourless chocolate soufflé torte, substitute the same amount of nut meal (almond, hazelnut, or pecan) for the flour. And if you're looking to serve the flourless version for Passover, skip the cardamom as well.

Ultra creamy and rich, with the soft, runny center of a molten chocolate soufflé, this fudgy cake is the ideal marriage of fancy and easy. You can top it with a blanket of whipped cream plus berries or chocolate shavings if you're looking for something grand and impressive. Or stick to a more minimalist approach with a plain dusting of cocoa powder or confectioners' sugar. It's perfect with coffee, tea, a big glass of milk, or a small glass of bourbon. In fact, it's just perfect, all around, and it even works as a gluten-free, Passover-ready dessert by using nut flour instead of all-purpose (see Swap It Out).

Note that if you only have a 9-inch springform pan, you can use it here, but the cake will be rather flat. Start checking for doneness after 22 minutes. Or you can use a regular 8-inch cake pan and serve the cake directly from it. Less elegant but just as delicious.

1. Heat the oven to 350°F. Butter an 8-inch springform pan and line the bottom with a round of parchment paper cut to fit.

2. In a large bowl, whisk together the sugar, cocoa powder, and salt. Pour the melted butter into the cocoa mixture and whisk until smooth.

3. Whisk the eggs into the mixture, one at a time, then whisk in the bourbon. Whisk in the flour until smooth and silky looking.

4. Scrape the batter into the prepared pan, smoothing the top. Bake until the top of the cake is just firm, the edges are puffed, and the center jiggles thickly, like Jell-O, when you shake the pan, 30 to 40 minutes. Err on the side of underbaking if you're not sure—this cake is better slightly underbaked than overbaked (the center should be a little runny when you cut it). Transfer the pan to a wire rack to cool completely, at least 2 hours.

5. Release the sides of the springform pan and remove them. Place the torte, still on the bottom of the pan, onto a platter. Just before serving, dollop the cake with whipped cream. Put 1 teaspoon or so of cocoa powder, along with a pinch or two of cinnamon, if you like, in a small sieve and shake over the cake to top it.

ONE-BOWL CAKES

No-Pots, Go-Withs & Basics

White Bean, Citrus, and Avocado Salad with Herbs

SERVES 4

2 teaspoons fresh lemon juice, plus more as needed

Pinch of crushed red pepper flakes

Kosher salt and freshly ground black pepper

2 tablespoons extra-virgin olive oil, plus more for serving

1 (15.5-ounce) can cannellini beans, drained and rinsed

1 small red onion, thinly sliced

2 large oranges (a combination of navel and blood is especially pretty)

1 small grapefruit

1 cup torn fresh parsley, mint, or cilantro leaves (or a combination)

2 tablespoons capers, drained and coarsely chopped

2 ripe Hass avocados, peeled, pitted, and sliced

Flaky sea salt, for serving

This colorful salad is juicy and sweet from the citrus, creamy and satisfying from the beans and avocados, and just a delight both to look at and devour. It makes a light meal on its own with some crusty bread, or a substantial side dish with simple roasted meats or fish. Try to find a brand of beans that contains salt. They have more flavor than unsalted beans and are better for salads.

1. In a large bowl, whisk together the lemon juice, red pepper flakes, a pinch of kosher salt, and a grind or two of black pepper, whisking until the salt dissolves. Whisk in the oil, then taste and add more kosher salt, if needed. The dressing should be well seasoned. Add the beans and onion and toss to combine.

2. **Supreme the citrus:** Cut the bottoms and tops off the oranges and grapefruit so the fruit is exposed and can stand upright on a cutting board. Using a paring knife, follow the curve of the fruit and cut away the peel and all the white pith. Working over the bean bowl to catch the juices, slice the segments out of their connective membranes and let them fall in with the beans.

3. Add the herbs and capers to the bean mixture, folding everything together. Taste and season with more kosher salt, black pepper, and lemon juice, if needed.

4. Fan the avocado slices out on a platter and season them lightly with kosher salt, then drizzle with a little oil and lemon juice. Spoon the bean and citrus mixture onto the platter, reserving the remaining dressing at the bottom of the bowl. Finish with flaky sea salt and a drizzle of oil, then spoon a little more dressing over the top.

VEG IT UP

If you'd like to serve this on a bed of greens, simply double the dressing and use enough of it to dress 4 to 5 ounces (4 to 5 cups) baby arugula or other salad greens. Put the greens on the platter first, then top with everything else.

Panzanella

with Tuna, Mozzarella, and Capers

SERVES 4 TO 6

2 pounds very ripe tomatoes
(a mix of varieties and colors
is nice)

3 ounces fresh mozzarella,
torn or cut into bite-size
pieces (½ cup)

½ cup thinly sliced red onion

1 garlic clove, finely grated

2 tablespoons red wine
vinegar, divided, plus more
to taste

1 tablespoon chopped
fresh basil

¼ teaspoon kosher salt, plus
more as needed

Freshly ground black pepper

Large pinch of crushed red
pepper flakes (optional)

¼ cup extra-virgin olive oil,
plus more as needed

½ cup thinly sliced Persian or
Kirby cucumber

½ cup torn fresh parsley
and cilantro leaves and
tender stems

4 ounces stale ciabatta or
baguette, cut into 1-inch
cubes (about 3 cups)

1 (5- to 6-ounce) can tuna,
preferably packed in olive oil,
drained

1 tablespoon capers, drained

This Tuscan bread salad is exactly the thing to make at the height of tomato season when there are a couple of overripe heirlooms oozing all over your countertop and it's just too hot to cook. Traditional panzanella is made from stale bread that's tossed with a dressing of sweet tomato juices, vinegar, and plenty of olive oil. This version also includes some mozzarella and tuna for richness and protein, along with cucumber for crunch.

1. Cut the tomatoes into bite-size pieces and put them in a large bowl. Add the mozzarella, onion, garlic, 1 tablespoon of the vinegar, the basil, a large pinch of salt, a grind or two of black pepper, and red pepper flakes, if using. Toss to coat and set aside.

2. In a medium bowl, combine the remaining 1 tablespoon vinegar, the ¼ teaspoon salt, and more black pepper. Whisk in the oil until well combined, then stir in the cucumbers and parsley.

3. Add the bread cubes, cucumber mixture, tuna, and capers to the tomatoes and toss well. Let sit for at least 30 minutes and up to 4 hours before serving. Toss with a little more oil, a little vinegar, and more salt and black pepper just before serving.

SWAP IT OUT

If you're using fresh rather than stale bread, you can toast it before putting it in the salad. Put the cubes on a rimmed sheet pan and drizzle with a couple tablespoons of olive oil and sprinkle with salt. Bake at 425°F for 7 to 10 minutes, until lightly browned. The toasted flavor is especially nice here.

VEGETARIAN UPGRADE

Skip the tuna and double the mozzarella.

Perfectly Adaptable
Green Salad

SERVES 4

1 tablespoon acid, such as fresh lemon or lime juice, or any kind of vinegar, plus more to taste

Fine sea salt and freshly ground black pepper

1 garlic clove, finely grated, or 1 tablespoon minced shallot, scallion, or other allium (optional)

1 teaspoon Dijon mustard (optional)

¼ cup extra-virgin olive oil, plus more as needed

8 cups (8 ounces) salad greens (any kind you like)

Not so much a recipe as a set of best practices, my go-to green salad evolves on a nightly basis, changing to accommodate whatever kind of fresh greens and other vegetables are available, and my mood for combining them. Mixing the acid and salt together before adding the olive oil gives the salt a chance to start dissolving, and I think makes for a more evenly seasoned salad. It's a slight but noticeable difference.

1. Put the acid and a pinch of salt in a salad bowl and whisk in some pepper, garlic, and mustard, if you like. Let the mixture sit for a minute or so to dissolve the salt and mellow out the pungency of the garlic.

2. Whisk in the oil a little at a time, until the dressing is well combined.

3. Add the salad greens and toss gently, preferably with your hands (this allows you to feel when the greens are coated with dressing without bruising them). Taste a green. Does it need a little more salt? A little more acid? Toss some in if so.

4. When the salad is delicious, serve it immediately or within 15 or 20 minutes of tossing. After that, it will start to wilt, especially the tender baby greens.

VEG IT UP

Add some sliced or cubed fresh vegetables to the salad bowl, whatever you've got, such as cucumbers, halved cherry tomatoes, mushrooms, bell peppers, thinly sliced sugar snap peas, celery, radish, turnip, carrot, or cooked or raw corn kernels. Make sure to add a little more salt, acid, and olive oil, if needed, to season all the vegetables.

Hands-Off Baked Polenta

SERVES 4 TO 6

2 to 4 tablespoons (¼ to ½ stick) **unsalted butter, cut into pieces,** or **extra-virgin olive oil,** plus more for the baking dish

4½ cups **vegetable or chicken stock** (or use water)

1½ cups **polenta (not instant)** or **coarse cornmeal**

1 teaspoon **fine sea salt** or **table salt,** plus more as needed

1 **bay leaf**

Grated Parmesan or pecorino Romano cheese, for serving (optional)

It does take longer to bake polenta than to simmer it on the stove, but what baking adds in time, it makes up for in ease of preparation. There's no splattering, no fear of lumps, and barely any stirring or monitoring at all. Just stick it in a 350°F oven for an hour or so, stirring it once halfway, and you're done. Once cooked, creamy polenta makes an excellent landing pad for any soupy, stew-y, or saucy dishes. Polenta will catch any excess liquid in the most delectable way.

1. Put an oven rack in the upper third of your oven and heat to 350°F. Generously grease a shallow 1½-quart casserole or gratin dish, or a 9 × 9-inch baking dish.

2. Pour the stock into the casserole dish, then stir in the polenta, salt, and bay leaf. Bake, uncovered, for 30 minutes. Using a fork, give everything a good stir and don't worry if the mixture looks separated at this point. Continue to bake, uncovered, until the polenta thickens somewhat and comes together, 25 to 35 minutes longer.

3. Remove the casserole dish from the oven and pluck out the bay leaf. Stir in the butter (adding more for extra richness, less to keep it leaner), cheese, if you like, and more salt to taste. Serve hot or warm.

Buttery No-Cook Couscous

SERVES 4 TO 6

1¾ cups boiling water (or use stock if you like)

1½ cups couscous (regular or whole wheat)

2 to 3 tablespoons butter (salted or unsalted)

½ teaspoon kosher salt

If you don't have an electric kettle, I'll admit this recipe is a bit of a cheat because you'll need a pot to boil the water. But even so, couscous is just about the easiest side dish there is beyond a loaf of crusty bread. And here, its nubby texture and buttery flavor makes it a low-key but genial partner to almost any main course.

1. In a large bowl, combine the boiling water, couscous, butter, and salt, and cover with a plate or pot cover. Let sit until the liquid is absorbed, 5 to 10 minutes.

2. Fluff with a fork and serve.

VEGAN UPGRADE

Use a good extra-virgin olive oil instead of butter.

ADD IT IN

Couscous loves company. When the liquid is absorbed, mix in chopped herbs, scallions or other alliums, diced tomatoes, a pinch or two of ground cumin or other spices, diced dried fruit like apricots or raisins, or toasted chopped nuts.

Homemade Chicken Stock

3 pounds meaty chicken bones (I like to use a combination of fresh chicken bones, such as backs, necks, and trimmings, plus some cooked bones leftover from roast chicken)

6 garlic cloves (you don't have to peel them but it's fine if they are already peeled)

5 to 7 fresh thyme sprigs or dill sprigs

5 to 7 fresh parsley sprigs

1 to 2 celery stalks

1 large carrot

1 large onion, halved but not peeled (or use 2 cups sliced leek greens)

1 tablespoon sea salt, or to taste

1 whole clove or star anise

1 bay leaf

1 teaspoon whole black peppercorns

2 to 4 (1-inch) coins fresh ginger (optional)

VEGAN UPGRADE

To make vegetable stock, follow the directions but skip the bones. Keep the aromatics the same and increase the vegetables—use 2 large onions, 4 carrots, 4 celery stalks, 2 tomatoes, and 8 ounces mushrooms. You can add a sheet of kombu to the broth as well.

Even though really good stock is becoming more available at supermarkets (check the freezer section), making it yourself is a worthwhile endeavor. It takes very little effort for something that really does make everything taste better. And it's extremely satisfying to use up all those kitchen scraps. I like to keep a bag of chicken bones and vegetable trimmings (parsley stems, leek greens, etc.) in the freezer. When it gets full, I know it's time to simmer up a pot of stock. Stock can be frozen for up to 6 months. I store mine in pint containers rather than quart. This gives me the most flexibility, and the defrosting goes more quickly.

1. Put the chicken bones, garlic, thyme, parsley, celery, carrot, onion, salt, clove, bay leaf, peppercorns, and ginger, if using, in a large stockpot, the pot of an electric pressure cooker, or a slow cooker. Cover everything with water. If using a stockpot, make sure the water covers the ingredients by 2 inches. If using an electric pressure cooker, add enough water so the ingredients are just covered. If using a slow cooker, they should be covered by an inch.

2. For a **stockpot**, bring everything to a simmer over high heat. Reduce the heat to low and let the stock simmer for 2 to 2½ hours, adding a little water if the liquid ever evaporates below the level of the bones and veggies. For an **electric pressure cooker**, seal the pot and cook on high pressure for 1 hour; either let the pressure release naturally or use the quick release (it doesn't matter). For a **slow cooker**, cook on low for 10 to 12 hours.

3. If you like, you can let the stock cool a bit before straining, 2 to 4 hours, uncovered. This makes it easier to deal with.

4. Put a strainer or colander over (or in) a large bowl. Pour the stock through it, pressing on the solids. Let the stock cool before storing. Stock can be refrigerated for up to 5 days, or frozen for up to 6 months.

Fail-Safe Rice

Here are two methods guaranteed to deliver a perfect pot of rice, whether you're using a pot on the stove or your electric pressure cooker on your counter. Of course, if you have a rice cooker, go ahead and use it, following the manufacturer's directions to get the best results.

Stovetop Method

MAKES 4 CUPS COOKED RICE

1½ cups any kind of white rice (long- or short-grain), rinsed very well

¼ teaspoon kosher salt

1. In a pot with a tight-fitting lid, combine 2¾ cups water, the rice, and salt. Bring the liquid to a boil over high heat.

2. Cover the pot, reduce the heat to maintain a low simmer, and cook for 17 minutes. Remove from the heat, place a clean kitchen towel between the top of the pot and the lid, and let stand for 10 minutes longer to steam (the towel absorbs the excess moisture, which makes for fluffier rice). Fluff with a fork before serving.

SWAP IT OUT

• To make brown rice on the **STOVE TOP**, use 3 cups water and cook for 40 to 50 minutes.

• To make brown rice in an **ELECTRIC PRESSURE COOKER**, cook on high pressure for 22 minutes, then let the pressure release naturally. Fluff and cover as directed in Step 4.

Electric Pressure Cooker Method

Yes, you can just press the rice button on your electric pressure cooker. But I think this method, which calls for steaming the rice with a kitchen towel on top to absorb the moisture, makes for fluffier rice.

MAKES 3 CUPS COOKED RICE

1 cup any kind of white rice (long- or short-grain), rinsed very well

¼ teaspoon kosher salt

1. In an electric pressure cooker, combine 1¼ cups water, the rice, and salt.

2. Seal the pot and set to cook on high pressure for 4 minutes for short-grain rice (such as Arborio or sushi rice) or 8 minutes for long-grain rice (jasmine or basmati).

3. Let the pressure release naturally for 10 minutes. Release the remaining pressure manually.

4. Fluff the rice with a fork, then cover the pot with a kitchen towel and put the lid back on (loosely, don't lock it in, or instead, you can place a plate on top of the kitchen towel). Let rest for 10 minutes before serving.

Acknowledgments

I'm forever grateful to the team that helped put this book together, because goodness knows I couldn't have done it without them.

My brilliant longtime editor, Doris Cooper.

My cheeky co-conspirator, Janis Donnaud (aka my agent).

The terrific folks at Clarkson Potter: Aaron Wehner, Raquel Pelzel, Francis Lam, Stephanie Huntwork, Kim Tyner, Bianca Cruz, Terry Deal, Kate Tyler, and Erica Gelbard.

The amazing photography team, including Linda Xiao and her assistant, Christina Zhang; food stylist Monica Pierini and her assistant, Emma Rowe; prop stylist Paige Hicks and her assistant, Julie Bernouis. What a fun shoot!

The best recipe testers ever, Jade Zimmerman, Adelaide Mueller, and Sofia Todesco.

And, as always, many thanks to my editors at *The New York Times* Food section, Sam Sifton, Emily Weinstein, and Krysten Chambrot. And to my recipe columnist colleagues, Genevieve Ko, Eric Kim, and Yewande Komolafe, who always inspire me in one-pot meals and beyond.

Finally, thanks to the very rascally Daniel and Dahlia. Wait, did you actually read this far?

Index